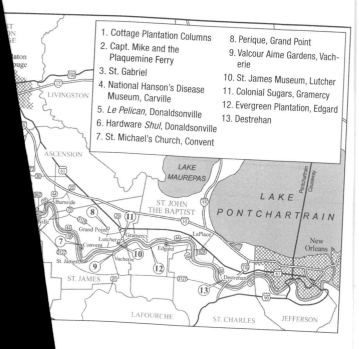

1. Cottage Plantation Columns
2. Capt. Mike and the Plaquemine Ferry
3. St. Gabriel
4. National Hanson's Disease Museum, Carville
5. *Le Pelican,* Donaldsonville
6. Hardware *Shul,* Donaldsonville
7. St. Michael's Church, Convent
8. Perique, Grand Point
9. Valcour Aime Gardens, Vacherie
10. St. James Museum, Lutcher
11. Colonial Sugars, Gramercy
12. Evergreen Plantation, Edgard
13. Destrehan

RA

The River Road
Between New Orleans and Baton Rouge

Map by Mary Lee Eggart

River Road RAMBLER

A Curious Traveler along Louisiana's Historic Byway

Mary Ann Sternberg

Illustrations by Elizabeth Randall Neely

Louisiana State University Press ❋ Baton Rouge

Published by Louisiana State University Press
Manufactured in the United States of America
First printing

Designer: Laura Roubique Gleason
Typeface: Calluna
Printer: McNaughton & Gunn, Inc.
Binder: Dekker Bookbinding

Frontispiece map by Mary Lee Eggart

Library of Congress Cataloging-in-Publication Data

Sternberg, Mary Ann.
    River Road rambler : a curious traveler along Louisiana's
historic byway / Mary Ann Sternberg; illustrations by Elizabeth Randall Neely.
        p. cm.
    ISBN 978-0-8071-5078-8 (cloth : alk. paper) — ISBN 978-
0-8071-5079-5 (pdf) — ISBN 978-0-8071-5080-1 (epub) —
ISBN 978-0-8071-5081-8 (mobi) 1. River Road (La.)—History.
2. River Road (La.)—History, Local. 3. River Road (La.)—Social life and customs. 4. Historic sites—Louisiana—River
Road. I. Neely, Elizabeth Randall. II. Title.
    F377.R58S85 2013
    976.3'3—dc23

                                                2012039194

The paper in this book meets the guidelines for permanence
and durability of the Committee on Production Guidelines
for Book Longevity of the Council on Library Resources. ⊚

CONTENTS

PREFACE

For the past two decades, I have rambled the River Road, which is my definition for making numerous leisurely excursions through this richly historic corridor. On most of these outings, I tried to pack a dedicated curiosity and a sense of humor to help me discover the character of the place. I found some locations and stories that seemed unique or, if not unique by the strictest definition, at least unusual and underappreciated—special treasures that intrigued me for a variety of reasons. So, with apologies to John Irving, this book may have been best titled *River Road Rambler: The World According to Me.*

Let me quickly define what I mean when I talk about the River Road, since my designation could seem a bit arbitrary. I am reclaiming here the definition I use in my book *Along the River Road:* it is the approximately one-hundred-mile-long corridor that traces the Mississippi River from the Jefferson/St. Charles parish lines up into East and West Baton Rouge Parishes. This cultural parkway, developed over three hundred years of recorded history, is layered with the settlements of many diverse people who have created a rich culture now bursting with local color. I didn't—and still do not—include the greater New Orleans area in my purview despite its extraordinary history and influence, only because so many fine and detailed books about the city already exist.

This book is a collection compiled by sifting through my two decades of rambling and learning about the area. This always came with surprises and the added advantage of an informal education about subjects far beyond my ordinary frame of reference. Many of these also offered almost as much local lore as formal history, which I did not resist.

The fifteen stories included in this collection seemed, through my personal prism, worth telling, although admittedly it was very difficult to decide what merited inclusion. Every plantation house open to the public is an extraordinary attraction; each small museum and the other diverse facilities that allow visitors to enjoy them are worth a stop. (All of these are identified and described in *Along the River Road,* third edition.)

Some of the places I wanted to write about don't offer public access, so I was delighted to be allowed escorted entrance after I'd convinced someone in charge about how compelling—and worth telling—their slice of the River Road is. Unfortunately, however, I was forced to omit a couple of subjects I had hoped to include, either because I couldn't find sufficient detail to present anything new or I was unable to gain entrance.

Originally I intended to write an historic essay about each subject, but somehow my observations and opinions intruded. The result is personal musings overlaid on a body of historic information, which may be a successful genre of writing or an utter failure. Nevertheless, it seemed the best way for me to tell these stories.

As these pieces reveal, I am partial to preservation: I love the relics of material culture as well as stories and traditions, believing they help define the meaning of the River Road. Through my years of rambling, I've been privileged to meet many people along the river who were deeply knowledgeable about their particular areas. They have tried to protect and honor the history and heritage around them and to provoke an interest by a broader public. I have relied for twenty years on these "keepers of the flame"—a term I learned from someone else who revered their dedication. Unfortunately, some of my keepers have died; many others have reached venerable ages and are no longer able to invest their time and energy into supporting the places they hold dear. So it is most gratifying when I've seen the work of these keepers appreciated and continued by a succeeding generation. It has been equally distressing when those who might be their logical heirs seem to have no appreciation for the value of the heritage around them, its tangible remains. In these cases, I fear that they expose River Road treasures to certain demise.

Beneath my preservationist instincts, however, also abides the core of a pragmatist. I know that the River Road is not a museum under glass but has been a place of constant change for three centuries. I enthusiastically embrace those changes that are thoughtful and might bring improvement and progress while valuing what is worthwhile and important. To me, both protection for its own sake and change without consideration of history are equally ill-advised.

Please ramble with me along the River Road and enjoy the stories I've chosen to tell. But do also go and trace this historic corridor for yourself because other stories are waiting to be told.

❧ I ❧

Sacred Spaces

1

Sacred Recycling

A friend made a point of taking me to St. Michael's Church in Convent. Behind the resplendent architecture, handsome paintings, and French hand-carved main altar of the main sanctuary was a small, quiet space that featured a grotto. "What do you see?" she asked with an impish grin. I looked around intently: five wooden benches facing the altar in the soft light of flickering votive candles; a running commentary of "thank yous" and "mercis," on small marble slabs lining the walls; four lovely tall and narrow stained-glass windows; and a high rock wall rising almost to the ceiling and filling the far end of the room. A statue of the Virgin Mary is tucked in an elevated niche within the wall, and another kneeling female statue is recessed in an alcove to the left of an odd-looking altar.

It was an Our Lady of Lourdes grotto, but I had no idea how unusual it was.

I'd had a vague notion of the story of Our Lady of Lourdes, much beloved by Catholics, which began with Bernadette Soubirous, the daughter of a miller in Lourdes, France, coming upon an apparition of the Virgin Mary on February 11, 1858. She had been collecting firewood near a rural cave when she saw "a young beautiful Lady clad in white with a blue sash, her feet bare but with a golden rose upon each foot." The Blessed Virgin Mary addressed Bernadette, saying, "I am the Immaculate Conception." Thereafter, despite her parents' prohibitions, Bernadette returned often to the cave to visit the apparition and, at the Virgin's request, dug in the ground and drank from the spring she found there. The spring created a pool of water, which, when given to ailing people, miraculously cured them. The apparition became known as Our Lady of Lourdes, and the place became a destination for pilgrims who presented prayers for help and were healed through taking the waters. Bernadette joined the Sisters of Charity, remaining a nun until her death in 1879. She was canonized in 1933.

Various replicas of the original Lourdes grotto exist around the world; most are cave-like openings or rock niches in which statues of the Virgin Mary have been placed. But the grotto at St. Michael's, originally constructed in 1876, is a bit different from the others, and not simply because it was one of the first created in the United States or because it may be the first grotto located inside a chapel.

Where else, my friend asked, would they have created a massive rock wall made of bagasse clinkers—the charred remains from burning the fibrous residue of sugarcane? And where else would the unseen support for the arch above the altar have been formed using an inverted sugar kettle—one of those broad, open metal cauldrons that were critical in nineteenth-century sugar processing and now decorate many Louisiana gardens? And when else will you see an altar totally studded with bright, pearlized clam shells from the river that are nailed in place to create the effect of an oddly textured mosaic?

The answer, of course, was nowhere else. This was a religious site uniquely and richly River Road.

St. Michael the Archangel Church was founded in 1809, a mile or so down the road from its present location, to give east-bank Catholics a place of worship without having to cross the river. The original building, small and modest, was replaced in 1831 with a striking brick edifice at the site of the present church. With its stepped gable façade and handsome bell cupola, it served the congregation well until the 1870s, when, all agreed, the congregation needed a larger, finer church. The project was supported, if not led, by the wise and revered Father Henry Bellanger, the parish priest. (Father Bellanger was also credited with the 1864 restoration of Jefferson College—now the Manresa Retreat Center—just down the road.) He had attended the Paris World Fair of 1867, where he had found the ornate wooden altar still in the main sanctuary. It's therefore possible that while in France, Father Bellanger might have visited, or at least heard much talk about, the miracles of Lourdes and the grotto to which believers had flocked for the past decade.

He may have brought this idea back to St. Michael's; however, he was reassigned to a church in New Orleans in 1870, leaving oversight of the building project to his successor, Father Onezine Renaudier. Renaudier had shared parish duties with Father Bellanger over the past three years and well understood what he envisioned.

Plans were formalized for the church renovations—a new rectory next door and improvements to the church building itself with the addition of two towers and a new sixty-foot steeple. (Easily seen by boats passing in the river, the steeple was a landmark until 1965, when the fierce winds of Hurricane Betsy toppled it.) The renovations would also include enhancing the church interior with two new sacristies and the grotto.

No documentation survives to indicate how the builders of the grotto were chosen, but according to Father Frank Uter who recently served in St. Michael's parish, church dynamics in the nineteenth century were probably similar to what they are today. The congregation would have formed a building committee and called on the respective talents of church members. In the 1870s, these would have included Jacques Joseph Florian Dicharry (known as Florian B.) and Christophe Colomb, Jr., the men credited with the grotto's design and construction.

Florian Dicharry was educated in architecture at MIT in Cambridge, Massachusetts, and returned to the Convent area to set up his practice. According to an 1890s photo, he was a handsome man with a full head of well-parted hair and a thin face that sported a walrus mustache and a small, shaggy goatee. He looked every bit the fine upstanding citizen he was, having gained a reputation not only as a respected architect (he later designed the steeple of St. Joseph's Cathedral in Baton Rouge) but also as a local civic leader, a director of the church school, and the owner of two short-lived local newspapers.

His partner, Christophe Colomb, was a grandson of the legendary River Road planter Marius Bringier and one of eight children of Christophe Colomb, Sr., a self-indulgent aesthete who had married one of the Bringier daughters and then given his wife license to run the family plantation while he pursued his interest in the arts. Junior, a dentist by profession, had apparently inherited his father's creativity; he dabbled successfully in engineering and experimented with various building materials, including bagasse. Colomb Jr.'s contemporaries described him as "an artistic builder and stone mason." He had garnered attention for his small, unorthodox plantation house, constructed with four pairs of columns along the front gallery that he'd rescued from another building. Because they were too tall for this reuse, he had dug out the earth instead of trimming them to size. Colomb had also added an enclosed belvedere above the second story of his home. Though I could never find a photograph of Colomb, I imagined him as a man with a twinkle in his eyes.

Nor could I find any official record of how the men divided up the grotto project, or whether they were personally friendly and had collaborated before or did so thereafter. Dicharry would have served as the architect for the church renovations and would have designed the grotto, but he is also credited with having personally nailed every clam shell to the wooden altarpiece. Colomb was responsible for the physical construction of the grotto and, considering his eccentricities, no doubt originated the concept of using bagasse and the other unorthodox construction elements.

Bagasse, the natural byproduct of milling sugar, is the refuse—stalks and leaves—left after the sugary liquid has been pressed from the cane. In the 1870s, bagasse was used to fuel furnaces, producing steam to power a sugar mill. Colomb had successfully experimented with it to produce an early version of wallboard as well as pillars, which he had applied to an outbuilding next to his eccentric home. Today, bagasse can still be used as fuel, and it is also commercially processed into insulation, wallboard, paper, and mulch.

Bagasse clinkers are the hardened remnants left in the grate or bottom of a furnace after the bagasse has been burned. They are created when impurities within the cane fibers—dirt, sand, and perhaps lime or potash—don't burn as do the fibers but are fused in the high heat of the furnace into various sizes of rock-hard nuggets. Clinkers are defined by sugar scientists at the LSU Audubon Sugar Institute as "the junk at the bottom." So Colomb's use of bagasse clinkers to fashion a wall resembling the cave grotto at Lourdes was both quirky and artistically inventive.

To build the wall, he created a support structure of brick and mortar, positioned the clinkers on it, and then fused them in place with cement. As a contemporary of Colomb's commented, "The grotto's superstructure looks and weighs like a meteor." Colomb is also credited with using the upturned sugar cauldron for the support framework of the arch above the altar. Though it is now unseen under the "rocks," the metal kettle would have been a familiar object to anyone living in sugarcane country. Colomb apparently recognized that, turned upside down, it would be a perfect component. Consequently, the size and shape of the arch were probably determined by which of the five standard sizes of sugar kettle he selected.

No documentation exists to reveal whether Colomb or Dicharry designed and constructed the wooden furniture of the altar or how they decided that instead of a standard altar finish of polished wood, theirs should be layered with artistically laid clam shells. They chose *Rangia cuneata* shells, a common local bivalve found in profusion along local waterways and in middens along the shores of nearby Lakes Pontchartrain and Maurepas.

Collecting enough shells would not have been difficult, but positioning them on the curved wooden planes of the altar and then separately nailing each one must have presented a challenge. Nevertheless, each shell was carefully placed and pinned by hand so that from the rear of the chapel, the altar appears to be covered with an odd white beading. Close up, however, there's no mistaking the dark nailhead centering each shell, creating the effect of thousands of tiny black eyes staring into the chapel.

These primitive finishes and the use of local materials have led contemporary visitors to suggest that the grotto chapel represents a form of folk art, particularly in contrast to the elegance and ornate decor of the main sanctuary. But ever since its dedication on Easter Sunday, April 17, 1876, the grotto and chapel have been a great source of pride to the parishioners of St. Michael's.

The dedication was attended by a huge crowd that watched a procession of eight church officials parade down the nave bearing the Virgin Mary statue to its new home in the niche high up in the wall of bagasse clinkers. Then the kneeling statue of Saint Bernadette saying the rosary was installed next to the altar. A brass band from Jefferson College played ceremonial music, and the occasion was noted as memorable and quite grand.

Because the grotto chapel has undergone some remodeling over the years, its appearance today is slightly different than at its dedication. Colomb's wall behind the grotto, originally exposed brick, was subsequently plastered over, and in the 1940s, Father Chauve, the resident priest, painted the plaster with rock formations, making the grotto seem to be part of a larger scene. Then, in 2004, a Milwaukee firm specializing in decorative painting and restoration was hired to update the chapel, replacing Father Chauve's artistry with a fresco of a mountain scene resembling the countryside around Lourdes. They cleaned the grotto and added a faux marbre finish to the wainscoting around the chapel. Celebration of these renovations included adding holy water to the chapel's fountain, brought back from Lourdes by Father Uter and Brennan Dicharry, one of Florian's descendants.

A ring of ex voto slabs, in thanks for favors granted, has grown throughout the years to well over one hundred since the first was donated in 1876. They are all anonymous with the exception of an early slab, donated by the family of local trapper Vasseur Weber, thanking the Blessed Mother for his safe return after four days lost in the swamp. Individual pilgrims still come to the grotto to pray for favors;

organized tours visit the chapel as well. But whenever I have been there, I've had the space to myself.

Since I'm not Catholic, I don't go to pray for favors. But I always offer thanks for Father Renaudier's inspiration and the creativity of his parishioners, Florian Dicharry and Christophe Colomb, Jr. They created something lasting and memorable, which could never exist anywhere else but the River Road.

2
Look What They Found!

The story of the old St. Gabriel Catholic Church reminds me of the best episodes of *Antiques Road Show,* the television program in which owners bring unidentified objects to an expert for evaluation. In the most dramatic instances, they are told they have a rare treasure. The owner's response is usually something like: My goodness, it's been collecting dust in my attic for decades! Who knew!!

I imagined that the church parishioners at St. Gabriel must have felt exactly the same way about their white clapboard Victorian church with the tall steeple and plain rose window. They had replaced it in 1953 with a large new place of worship, leaving the building as a charming landmark along the River Road.

Later, however, after architectural historians began to poke about, it was revealed that the lovely nineteenth-century church was actually a renovated Spanish colonial building dating from the late eighteenth century. The church had been constructed by the early Acadian settlers lured to the area by the Spanish government, a defending presence against the British who were located just upriver. Furthermore, the architectural sleuths agreed, the St. Gabriel church might be the only surviving church building from that period in all of the Mississippi Valley—a rare treasure. My goodness, the parishioners might have exclaimed, it's been sitting here looking country-Gothic for as long as any of us can remember. Who knew!!

Who would have known either then or now, for although a historic marker in front of the church offers a capsulized version of its history, the exterior of the building belies none of it. When I couldn't imagine the building as anything other than what I saw, I made an appointment to visit it in the company of one of its ardent supporters (something anyone can do) to see its history for myself.

The simple interior looked just as it has since the 1871 renovation, with the addition of decorative clumps of dust and trails of cobwebs. The church nave, defined by board walls and a low-arched cathedral ceiling, was covered in dusky mint-green burlap, artfully stenciled; two rows of slim white columns defined the center aisle along a natural pine plank floor, and four simple lancet-topped windows on each side offered a view out to God's world.

But I couldn't know what I was looking at until my knowledgeable guide pointed out distinguishing elements of the original architecture. The church, he reminded me, was completed the same year that the Declaration of Independence had been written by representatives of the original thirteen American colonies. He lifted a pine board to reveal a broad hand-hewn plank, a piece of the original flooring, and shined a light into the exposed attic that had been made visible where a ceiling corner had been pried away. With the flashlight beam, he traced the lines of the sturdy eighteenth-century, Norman-truss cypress framing.

He encouraged me to feel the texture of an exposed hand-planed, cypress wall beam; it was more than nine feet tall and nine inches thick, making our contemporary framing timbers look like flimsy matchsticks. He also pointed out the puzzle-piece fit of mortise and tenon joints in a wall bared to show them. Equally surprising, he showed me that the country-Gothic windows were positioned exactly where the window openings had been when the Acadians had worshipped in the building in the eighteenth century.

He knew all this because he was among a small group of devoted local historians who had painstakingly researched and recreated the story of the Acadians' church, then exhibited what they'd discovered. Their discoveries are revealed through an assortment of texts, drawings created by architects, early photographs of the country-Gothic church, and three-dimensional models of what the Acadians' house of worship would have looked like, all placed unceremoniously around the church interior. They are instructive to anyone interested in the old building's history and construction, and they show how a group of keepers of the flame solved the mystery about a unique old building that was misunderstood for so many years.

The community of St. Gabriel was established in 1767, when the Spanish colonial government lured Acadian exiles to the area with an offer of free land. The settlers were probably disappointed to discover they were not joining friends already established nearby but were instead being sent to the Manchac District to help strengthen the Spanish fort, San Gabriel, that was positioned on the Mississippi River at the convergence with Bayou Manchac, just across from the fort of their British enemies.

The Acadians' new settlement was over two miles distant from the fort as the crow flies rather than adjacent to it. This location may have been chosen because it was out of the reach of cannon shot; the selected site also claimed the first straight stretch of Mississippi River below the fort, as the land next to the fort formed a cape or point—now called as Plaquemine Point—that was too narrow to be encircled by the standard land grants of forty arpents' depth. So the settlement that would become the community of St. Gabriel was strung out along this stretch of riverbank, with each lot given a small river frontage and forty arpents' depth, including the lot specified as the site for a Catholic church.

Until 1971, no one seemed to know what had happened to the Acadians' church. But that year, an architect hired to refurbish the country-Gothic church building noticed construction oddities as he poked about the attic. He told local historian and parishioner Eugene LeBlanc that the building framing seemed unusual; it looked as if it had come from two different buildings.

Not long afterward, historic architect Sid Gray, also curious about the church's provenance, began to explore. Gray had acquired a reputation for architectural sleuthing and was renowned for his predilection for unselfconsciously crawling under buildings and climbing through attics in search of "the bones of the building." After Gray studied the flooring, joists, and rafters of the old church, he knew it was unusual. The attic beams had been cut away to allow installation of the neo-Gothic cathedral ceiling, but he could tell that, had the framing been complete, it would once have formed a cut-timber Norman truss supporting a double-pitched roof. This would have extended beyond the church interior to cover an exterior gallery encircling the building. These "bones" were clues—the distinctive elements of an eighteenth-century colonial design used in the French Creole style of construction.

The church was, in fact, the building of the Acadians, disguised under a country-Gothic renovation. Other experts concurred.

Local lore had long held that the Acadians' church had been originally constructed in 1769 near the fort and later moved to the settlement. To test this theory, in 1991 David Broussard, an expert wood craftsman and conservator, decided to remove a few pieces of exterior siding and peek into the church walls. If the church had been moved, he knew it would show evidence of partial reconstruction and more than one set of nail holes. Instead, he found twelve-inch-wide, overlapping, hand-sawed beveled boards bearing only one set of nail holes, confirming that not only was the church original, but also that it had been at approximately the same location since the settlers drove its last nail in 1776.

Gene LeBlanc, David Broussard, and others have spent decades learning about the colonial settlement of St. Gabriel and its church by studying detailed Spanish colonial records. They have pieced together a fascinating, true-as-possible story, complete with snippets about settler foibles. Acadian settler Pierre Babin, for example, had been originally assigned a lot in the St. Gabriel community, but it was appropriated instead in 1770 for the site of the church. Babin complained to the authorities; he had already cleared the lot. He was obviously displeased. The commandant was duly apologetic, subsequently compensating him for his effort and giving him another lot.

By 1772 the settlers had nearly completed a presbytere (the residence of the priest) and twenty-seven homes, which meant that sixty of the assigned lots were still empty. That included the lot allocated for the church, which was still just a promise.

Construction on the Acadians' house of worship finally began in 1774. It was designed by Louis Andry, an engineer for the Spanish colonial government; Louis LeConte of LaFourche, a settlement across the river (now Donaldsonville), supervised construction. The Acadian settlers themselves took up hammers and nails in the hours between farming and other tasks necessary for sustaining their lives in the wilderness. By the fall of 1776, the church had been completed; it measured 60 feet in length by 33-1/2 feet in width and was surrounded by dirt-floored galleries. "It is very beautiful," Commandant Louis Dutisne enthusiastically wrote to the Spanish governor. Despite its beauty, however, the congregants waited for three years for assignment of a permanent pastor.

In 1818, the church apparently underwent its first remodel after having been set, or rolled, back. "Rolling back" was a common practice along the Mississippi River before the uniform levee was built. It was a way to protect structures from encroaching water, accomplished by placing logs beneath a building and literally rolling it farther back on its property. This particular move appears to have been the origin of the mistaken belief that the church had been moved from near the fort. Architectural historians surmise that the front gallery survived this move but that the side and rear galleries were stripped off to facilitate the process and never restored. This oversight would eventually expose the once-protected cypress side walls to the elements, hastening some physical deterioration to the building.

When the hardships of the Civil War came to Louisiana, parishioners would have been able to pay less attention to their church and money was tight. After the war, as the community reorganized, there may have been a desire to make the church look more progressive, which would have motivated the congregation to agree to the 1871 church renovation in the then-popular country-Gothic style.

The refurbishment lowered the height of the nave with the addition of the pine cathedral ceiling, which was held up by the trim white columns. It also extended the length of the building, to the rear to accommodate a new altar flanked by a pair of sacristies and to the front with the addition of the tall rose-windowed steeple.

Meanwhile, geography and climate took their toll. The "new" church was forced to roll back again in 1887 because of river encroachment; in 1909, it suffered damages in a hurricane, which led to the recovering of the interior walls with the decorative stenciled burlap. Again in 1932, the building was moved back, parking it finally where it remains today.

Beyond these sketchy details, however, little more is known about the church because its records were lost at the time of the renovation, possibly destroyed in a flood. So no paper trail remains to document why the architecture of the church was changed or who cut the Norman truss from the attic and repositioned many of the old beams and joists to other parts of the building where they have subsequently been found. What is known about church history has been by pieced together from other sources.

But the condition of the church and the new understanding of its history is pretty convincing, David Broussard told me. Often, so much has been added to a building that its original footprint is hard to ascertain, or its interior is dramatically reconfigured with repositioned windows and doorways. Not so in the old St. Gabriel church. Its outline is really little changed, and most of the original structure—beams, posts, and joists—have been retained within the building, even if some were creatively repositioned.

The keepers of the flame continue to argue among themselves about what is best for their historical project: should the old St. Gabriel Church be restored to its eighteenth-century appearance if funding were available? Should it be formalized as a museum? Or should it remain just as is, with its eighteenth-century bones informally revealed under its nineteenth-century form?

I don't take sides in this argument, although it would be a great addition to the River Road if the interior were renovated as a museum and the collection organized to tell the building's story to visitors. The old church deserves to be acknowledged for its place in Louisiana history and architecture. Yet the church building as it is now tells its own story, simply requiring a keeper of the flame to help translate.

These days, when I pass by the old St. Gabriel church, I'm inclined to scowl a bit at the cramped plate of its historic marker because, as I now know, its text reveals so little of the building's remarkable story.

3

The Hardware *Shul*

Shul: *a Yiddish word, translates as "a Jewish house of worship and prayer, a synagogue."*

The Ace Hardware store sits tight on the corner of Railroad Avenue and Nicholls Street in Donaldsonville's old downtown. And if you look closely, you can't miss seeing that the building is an odd juxtaposition of architectural styles: a 1950s, one-story, shed-roofed commercial facade covers the lower level of a tall, buckskin-colored, wood-frame building with an eave decorated with white gingerbread trim. It is clear that this building has a checkered, if indecipherable, history.

I pushed my way through the glass front doors into a typical hardware store. Metal columns supported a low ceiling, shelves were crammed, and the walls were hung with a standard assortment of offerings to fix, build, and improve. Squarely in front of the entrance was Aisle 2, headed by a squat lazy-Susan, its pie-wedged bins brimming with nails. Beyond it were shelves stacked with flashlights, locks, castors, precariously balanced packs of light bulbs, reams of sandpaper, and much more. But I hadn't come here to shop.

I knew that this building at 301 Railroad Avenue had originally been the Bikur Cholim Synagogue, Donaldsonville's long-time—and only—Jewish house of worship, now regarded as the oldest surviving synagogue building in the state. I came, curious to discover what that building had looked like and was hoping to envision what it was like when Donaldsonville was the home of a small but thriving Jewish community.

Once inside the store, however, I quickly realized that it would take a better imagination than mine to discern elements of a house of prayer among the hammers and nails. I had deduced from a 1925-era photograph of the synagogue that Aisle 2 would probably have tracked the synagogue's main (perhaps only) aisle. It would have extended from just inside the entry through the sanctuary and would have ended at the bimah, the raised platform where rabbis and lay leaders conducted services and where the Ark, the receptacle for Torah scrolls, would have been located on its back wall.

I scanned the interior of the hardware store wondering if the bimah might have been located just beyond the small lighted exit sign that hung at the rear of the selling floor. I approached the earnest young clerk behind the front counter. What did he know about the old synagogue, I asked, and received his honest reply: virtually nothing. But he was kind enough to humor my request to look beyond the exit sign, where I saw only a small back foyer. A pair of large old double doors painted brick-red opened into a small backyard, and a cluttered storeroom was to the right of the foyer; a staircase rose against the wall on the left. I could see nothing at all that seemed to betray the existence of a synagogue.

At my obvious disappointment, the clerk acknowledged that I was not his first dissatisfied Jewish pilgrim; others had come to the store looking for traces of the old synagogue too. But that was hardly surprising: a circuit known as Cultural Corridors, a southern Jewish heritage trail, is mapped from New Orleans to Memphis and includes two Donaldsonville destinations—the 1877 elegant Italianate building in downtown Donaldsonville that had housed the B. Lemann and Brothers department store and the Bikur Cholim cemetery, still in place since its establishment in 1856. The old synagogue building is no longer considered a landmark.

* * *

"The new Jewish synagogue is being rapidly completed," the *Donaldsonville Chief* reported in 1871. The following year an enthusiastic article reported the occasion of the synagogue's dedication. Bikur Cholim is "a commodious, tall structure built of wood with Victorian style filigree trimming the roofline and a double archway over the entry," the *Chief* recounted. "[There is] a rosette window but no other decoration [and] a small balcony on the second floor."

Rabbi H. S. Jacobs from the Carondelet Synagogue in New Orleans conducted an impressive dedication ceremony, the *Chief* noted, as a permanent rabbi had not yet been engaged. Rabbi Jacobs "repeated the customary dedicatory phrases alternately in Hebrew and English, [with] the [well-known local] Silver Cornet Band filling up the pauses with solemn music." The article, however, failed to include a roster of those in attendance, even though the ceremony would surely have claimed the attention not only of the area's Jewish residents but also many non-Jewish dignitaries and friends. Donaldsonville's small Jewish community was held in high regard. "Our Jewish residents are reckoned among the best and most liberal-minded citizens and are associated with every progressive move," the *Chief* effused in 1900. Over time, several of those citizens served as mayors of the city.

Bikur Cholim attracted members not only from Donaldsonville proper but also from towns along Bayou Lafourche—Napoleonville, Plattenville, and Klotzville. In its most active period, in fact, the little Donaldsonville synagogue was the largest Jewish congregation between New Orleans and Baton Rouge. It held regular services on Friday nights and Saturday mornings, Sunday school for its children, and celebrated life-cycle events, some of which made the social pages of the *Chief.* The newspaper complimented the ladies of the synagogue for organizing successful benefit fairs and elegant fundraising balls, and it dedicated column inches to the marriage of Jacob Lemann's daughter and the bar mitzvah of his grandson. (Jacob Lemann was prominent not only as Donaldsonville's first Jewish resident but also as one of the most successful businessmen and landowners in the parish.)

In 1878, Charles Wesslowsky, representing a national Jewish

organization on a tour of southern Jewish communities, stopped in Donaldsonville. He reported it was "one of the most flourishing little cities in the state" and admired its Jewish citizens—"good and worthy conductors"—and its "handsome new synagogue with its polished and intelligent leader, Rev. Dr. Sophar." Wesslowsky also offered cheers for the synagogue's energetic volunteer choir and commended its flourishing Ladies' Hebrew Benevolent Society.

If Wesslowsky had found a vibrant community, however, within a decade of his visit Bikur Cholim was forced to undergo reorganization. It must have done so successfully, for congregants hired Rabbi Marx Klein as the new rabbi. He led services and taught Hebrew classes and Sunday school until his retirement in 1905. Thereafter, the congregation never again had a resident rabbi, relying instead on visiting clergy or laymen to lead the congregation's religious activities.

Bikur Cholim, like many synagogues in small southern communities, had begun to falter because it lost its next generation. As they did in many other small towns, some of Donaldsonville's young Jewish natives fled to life in bigger cities with larger Jewish populations. But in Donaldsonville, the loss was accelerated by the large number of intermarriages between Jews and Catholics, whose children were all raised in the Catholic Church.

Synagogue membership, which once numbered more than eighty, with as many as one hundred and fifty in attendance at a service or an event, diminished so dramatically that by the 1940s there were too few practicing Jews to hold weekly services. Members still gathered twice a year—to observe Rosh Hashanah (the Jewish New Year) and Yom Kippur (the Day of Atonement), but it had become increasingly apparent that there were neither congregants nor funding to sustain the synagogue.

In 1954, the painful decision was made: the building on Lot 166, Square 42, with its 68-foot front footage on Railroad Avenue, must be sold. It was in the prime commercial district and was quickly purchased by two local non-Jewish doctors. The sanctuary was deconsecrated; its Torah and religious artifacts were distributed to other Jewish congregations, and the proceeds from the sale were placed into a perpetual care fund for the benefit of the Bikur Cholim cemetery. The doctors converted their building into a Western Auto store and added the commercial façade.

All of these details of Bikur Cholim's history were well documented when I began what became a quest to figure out what the synagogue had looked like. I considered it a somewhat oblique way to honor the memory of Jewish Donaldsonville. But it soon seemed as if I'd missed my opportunity; in a twenty-year-old interview with Gaston Hirsch, the last, longtime Jewish resident of Donaldsonville, a reporter followed Hirsch around the hardware store, noting where the bimah had been—"where the epoxy and paint cans are"—and the pews—"where the reels of electrical wire are." Hirsch lamented that the synagogue's beautiful windows were gone. But I never met Mr. Hirsch before he died and his descriptions did not fit the store's current interior at all.

I sought clues to the synagogue from descendants of Jacob Lemann, local historians, and old-timers unrelated to the Jewish community who I hoped might have been in the synagogue for some reason. But after speaking with innumerable people, studying stacks of documents, and scouring old newspaper articles and a variety of archives, I had discovered virtually nothing further.

And then, just as I had determined to abandon what I now was beginning to consider a quixotic pursuit, I was unexpectedly introduced to Mark Gautreau, the owner of the Ace Hardware store. He had bought the old building from Western Auto in 1977, restocking its interior and, in 1985, had moved with his family into a space he reconfigured above the store.

Mark Gautreau was too young to have seen the original interior of the synagogue and had never seen a photograph of it. He was, however, an accomplished woodworker who had framed up his family living quarters in the attic of the building. As a craftsman, he had noted the skillful details of its construction. "Every finger joint is precise, braced . . . and all the studs are forty-foot-high heart [of] pine," he effused. It was the framing of the old synagogue.

He had also perceived the outlines of the synagogue's four tall windows along each side, which are distinct in the 1925 photograph I'd seen. He led me into a narrow side garden where he pointed out barely perceptible outlines of the original windows, filled in so expertly that they melded almost perfectly into the siding. He pointed up to the second floor, where artistic transoms decorated the windows of his residence. Those were the original transoms, he told me; he had salvaged them, had them artistically retrofitted with shards of blue glass, and reinstalled them for his new home.

The hardware store's commercial façade and low ceiling had been added by the owners of Western Auto, but Gautreau understood construction enough to know that they had probably moved the synagogue's front doors to the back foyer—those brick-red, double doors I'd seen on my first visit. However, I hadn't noticed a narrow scuffed wall to the right of the large doors—a short run of wainscoting almost six feet high with a high plastered wall above it. This, Gautreau surmised, had been painted white and was the sole remaining section of the synagogue's original interior walls.

We climbed the stairway to his apartment on treads and risers crafted of natural cypress that had the slightly creaky, tight feel of old-fashioned carpentry. This staircase, Mark Gautreau suggested, was the original one to the synagogue's balcony. Perhaps when Western Auto lowered the ceiling, they had removed the stairs to the back foyer, giving them easy access to the cavernous attic they'd created to use as a warehouse.

The stairs opened onto a large living area. It was roomy and airy under a tall, shallow, barrel-vaulted ceiling constructed of old pine boards, painted white, which ran the length of the room. A graceful, curved board molding connected the ceiling to the high walls of the room, making a gracious space in proportion and simplicity. This was part of the unfinished attic Mark Gautreau found above the selling floor of Western Auto, and he'd simply refurbished it—the synagogue's original ceiling.

But his special pride was reserved for the softly burnished, longleaf pine flooring which he'd found as the floor of the Western Auto store. He had pried up the boards, sanded them clean of layers of paint, and refinished them to expose the beautiful grain of the old wood. "Tongue-in-groove and six-inch-wide," he grinned. It was the synagogue's original flooring.

I was beginning to be able to envision the original space.

Not long after Mark Gautreau had shown me these architectural details, a woman I didn't know named Caroline Masur found me. Someone had told her I was looking for information on the old synagogue. She was quick to warn me that she was now "of a certain age," which made her memory less than perfect. But she had grown up in Klotzville and had attended services at Bikur Cholim with her family until she was a young teen. Yes, she told me, a carpeted center aisle had reached from the double front doors to the bimah, but the rest of the synagogue floor had been bare pine planks. She remembered scuffing her shoes on that floor as she sat, not always attentively, on a cushion in the dark, polished wood pews decorated with scrolled backs.

The sanctuary ceiling was very high, she remembered, lit by lights that hung down on long chains. And there were four large windows of clear but textured glass on each side wall; they admitted sunlight but frustratingly smudged the view of the world outside. The bimah had been raised and carpeted, simply furnished with a lectern for the rabbi and two high-backed pulpit chairs for readers or synagogue members; the ark on the bimah wall holding the Torah was an unadorned cabinet with wooden doors. She wished she knew what had become of the Torah or the synagogue's religious artifacts when the congregation had disbanded.

I was elated with my chance encounters and the details I had garnered about Bikur Cholim synagogue. I admit it was hardly comparable to the discovery of the Dead Sea Scrolls by Bedouin shepherds or to Hiram Bingham's uncovering Machu Picchu. But in the same way that archeologists build stories about how people lived based on the objects they discover at a site, I considered these construction clues and memories the best way currently possible to reconstruct a sense of the synagogue. They are not irrefutable, of course, but I have visited a number of rural synagogues throughout the South and there are many similarities. What I learned from Mark Gautreau and Caroline Masur seems believable.

That means that, despite the clutter of stock in Ace Hardware, I can now visualize the building as it was when families from Donaldsonville, Plattenville, and Klotzville arrived through the large double front doors to participate in the rites of Judaism. They walked down the center aisle and took their seats in cushioned dark wood pews. The sanctuary was a simple and elegant space, with natural plank flooring and walls of tall board wainscoting rising as high as the base of the tall windows. I can picture the lofty ceiling gently arching overhead and the sounds of a volunteer choir, who climbed the cypress stairway and sang prayers and hymns that resounded throughout the sanctuary.

Perhaps someone more imaginative than I am will also be able to feel the presence of those generations who animated the space then. For now, I am satisfied with construction clues and faded memories to appreciate something of what the Bikur Cholim Synagogue offered, before its building became a retail store in a town that has no more Jewish residents.

II

Elegant Evidence

4
For the Life of a Garden

*Francois Gabriel Aime, born in 1797, was nicknamed "Valcour" by
a family nurse. He married Josephine Roman and the couple lived
with the bride's widowed mother. Valcour bought a nearby property on which to build their own home, but when Mrs. Roman Sr.
died, Josephine's second brother, Jacques Telesphore, inherited her
plantation. Valcour acquired it from him, leaving Jacques with
the tract that is now the famed Oak Alley Plantation.*

*Valcour and Josephine spared no expense in refurbishing, en-
larging, and furnishing their home. In 1842, with input from his
wife, he began planning an extraordinary garden. Soon, Aime was
renowned for it. Following the death of his son Gabriel in 1853,
however, the tycoon sank into despair. With the succeeding deaths
of his wife and two daughters, he sank into a depression, ceased
having an interest in the garden, and turned over his business to a
son-in-law. Valcour Aime died in 1867.*

*John Burnside of Houmas House Plantation subsequently pur-
chased the Aime Plantation for its sugar property, paying no attention to either the grand house or its extraordinary garden.*

Scott unlocks a rusty iron gate nestled into a crumbling brick pil-
lar and waves me through the wedged opening. We're on private

property that happens to be his. The gray chill of the day exaggerates the dull palate of the landscape as we begin to bushwhack through brown and tan and muted green, clambering over fallen trees and picking through tangles of vines that have woven themselves into netting among the dense overgrowth. We should, he mutters, keep a wary eye out for snakes.

I'd seen this place from the River Road many times, a stand of trees encircled within the unbroken lines of cane fields. It looked like a wilderness, more suitable for hiking with the Sierra Club than the site of a legendary nineteenth-century garden created and owned by the equally legendary sugar baron, Valcour Aime. But here it is, a ten-and-a-half acre footprint within a protective fence, the most tangible vestige of the grand lifestyle of Valcour Aime, who was known as a wildly successful planter, experimenter in sugar processing, and bon vivant. He called his property the St. James Refinery Plantations but others referred to it, apparently without malice, as "Le Petit Versailles."

Nothing remains of the resplendent Aime mansion; it burned in 1920, reducing to ash what was left of the three grand staircases, checkerboard marble floors, and dining room fashioned after one at the Château de La Rochefoucauld in France. It had been in that very room, in fact, that one of the best-known stories about Valcour Aime was born. According to lore, Aime wagered a dinner guest from France the then-princely sum of $10,000 that everything presented on the gold table service at his table had come from his property— from the turtle, wild fowl, vegetables, salads, and fruits to the coffee, cigars, wines, and liqueur. When the guest challenged his host on bananas, coffee, and tobacco, Aime shepherded him through the plantation's carefully tended conservatories and hothouses and duly accepted his winnings.

In the 1840s and 1850s, the River Road was one of the richest regions of the country. Neighboring plantations were gloriously enhanced with oak alleés, formal landscaping, and thick groves of orange trees, but Valcour Aime dreamed of something entirely different. He wanted to transform the land between his house and the Mississippi River into what landscape architects today call a jardin d'anglais-chinois—an English garden with Chinese influences, a popular style in England and on the Continent in the mid-nineteenth century. In an 1842 diary entry, Aime noted that the ground was being prepared "for an English park."

The resulting landscape was unlike any other American garden of the period. It was enclosed within a high brick wall lined with fragrant shrubs. A massive iron entryway from the River Road opened onto a broad shell driveway leading to the house, which was crisscrossed by other smaller drives. Discrete gardens and sweeps of lawn had been created to appear informal and natural. Interspersed throughout were water features—a manmade stream and ponds fed by water pumped from the Mississippi—and follies such as a small mountain, a grotto, a fortress, and a pagoda.

Aime hired a master gardener, Joseph Miller, whose plantings included not only local flora but also exotic plants imported from Korea, India, Cuba, and Madagascar. The latter were for beauty and effect but also to engage Aime's love of experimentation: he was interested to determine which exotics might be adaptable to the south Louisiana climate. Growing about the grounds and in the conservatories were roses, wisteria, Confederate jasmine, clematis, lilies, bleeding heart, heliotropes, and mahonia; sweet olive and magnolia fuscata; camphor, cedar, white walnut, magnolia, and Chinese parasol trees; peaches and bananas; a grove of orange trees and kumquats trees; and more. Some accounts have also mentioned a noteworthy zoological collection—exotic fish swimming in the ponds, imported game birds, songbirds, peacocks strutting the grounds, swans gliding along the water, even white gazelles and kangaroos—although the latter, at least, were probably fanciful.

Eliza McHatton Ripley visited Aime's daughter Felicié in 1847 when both girls were young teenagers. Eliza Ripley's girlhood remembrance of the garden appeared in her book *Social Life in Old New Orleans,* published in 1910, which remains the best first-person account of the garden in its glory. She described "a miniature river, meandering in and out and around the beautifully kept parterres, the tiny banks of which were an unbroken mass of blooming violets. A long-legged man might have been able to step across this tiny stream but it was spanned at intervals by bridges of various designs, some rustic, some stone, but all furnished with parapets so one would not tumble in. There were summer houses draped with strange, foreign looking vines; a pagoda on a mound, the entrance of which was reached by a flight of steps. It was an octagonal building with stained-glass windows and struck [me] as a very wonderful and surprising bit of architecture. Further on was a mountain covered from base to top with beds of blooming violets. A narrow winding path led to the summit from which a comprehensive view was obtained of the extensive grounds, bounded by a series of conservatories."

Garden professionals of the era came to visit Aime's masterpiece, pronouncing it one of the finest botanical gardens in America. A botanical collector who visited there in 1849 deemed it "not surpassed, if equaled, by any in the Union."

Although nothing of this nineteenth-century opulence remains, Valcour Aime's garden continues to be of interest to landscape architects because it is a rare first-generation garden. Unlike most historic gardens, which are benevolently updated through the years, beneath its century of wild growth the garden of Valcour Aime retains its original layout; it has never been altered, improved, restored, or updated since 1853, when the clock figuratively stopped. For a short time thereafter, the master gardener and thirty slaves maintained the property but did nothing more to introduce plants or garden features. Any alteration to the garden since then has been only by subtraction—original plants dying or naturalizing beyond their initial sites, invasive species taking root, and loss to theft in the early years by vandals and romantics who poached plants, pieces of fountains, and portable decoration.

The deterioration of the abandoned garden was documented through the years by assorted visitors. Catherine Cole (the pseudonym of *Times-Picayune* reporter Martha Field) came in June 1892 and saw the crumbled remains of an old brick wall near the River Road, over which "had been spiked the iron bars and iron columns of a fence. Far away (through a tangle of bramble and bloom) huddled the stately, solitary half-ruined home. All above the tangled garden grew vines luxuriantly, as if in haste to knit a tapestry of secrecy and awe."

She stood on the gallery of the house with Andrien, "a stout-knit, sad-faced Negro with a beard," who told her he had lived on the plantation for fifty-one years and was then caretaker and its last resident. As Andrien looked out over the garden area, he reminisced about the banana grove, a pineapple house near the big camphor tree, and a cactus house, adding that once "we had eighteen gardeners." He told Catherine Cole that his heart was broken "to see the vines like cobwebs, the gloom, the rain," and she in turn departed in a state of melancholy, thinking of the place as "the grand old museum and its garden of dead delights."

By the time author Herman Seebold visited the garden in 1941, it was completely derelict. He wrote that "in the midst of an ancient grove of old oaks dying from neglect," underbrush had claimed the site of the home. He saw only "crumbling brickwork, outlines of old flowerbeds once filled with a riot of costly plants, marble statuary, fountains, winding walks, streams and grottoes—all densely hidden in a thick growth that forms a wilderness. [Still], among the trees and underbrush one still can find traces of many garden conceits, broken marble urns, stained and crumbling marble garden benches, parts of old fountains of which there were many about the grounds, and parts of an old masonry bridge of elaborate design near the ruins of an old gazebo."

A decade later, Lyle Saxon picked his way "through the maze," noting how difficult it was to believe that "once upon a time, this ground was known far and wide as Le Petit Versailles." And Harnett Kane, who always wrote with the eye of a romantic, lamented that "enough is there to give a sad hint of the lost glories."

But not everyone considered the place without promise. A 1959 study of the River Road by the U.S. Department of Commerce suggested that the garden might be a site for development as a "day-use area with woodland trails and facilities for picnicking," a concept abhorrent to anyone who valued the history of the tract.

As Scott and I thrash through the thickets, we are quite aware that we are inside a landscape that still bears the imprint and spirit of Valcour Aime. We head to the little riviere, now much wider than in

Eliza Ripley's memory, because this will offer an easier path by which to explore some of the property. The channel of the waterway is dry and carpeted with a lush layer of dead leaves, but it is no less an obstacle course of felled trees, ropey vines, and wild shrubs. Soon we round a gentle bend and I spy the remnants of a bridge arching across the channel. I've brought a diagram from an old study of the garden with me and see that this is called the Roman bridge. Its parapet wall is gone, reducing the bridge to a brick arch wearing a crown of green moss, decorated with saplings wreathed in swirls of ivy rising from its deck. A photograph of the bridge taken in 1940 showed much more of the parapet in place. Now, fallen chunks of brick lie in the channel, looking as if they've been there for decades.

The bank of the little river is lined with bright green ferns and occasional clumps of Louisiana iris. Do they date from Aime's time or have they volunteered in a hospitable environment? Since it's not the season for blooming violets, I can't tell if Eliza Ripley's unbroken mass of purple might remain.

Farther along, a second bridge crouching over the streambed comes into view. This one is made of stones or something resembling stone, and it is also dappled with patches of bright green moss. To its left are the remains of Valcour Aime's folly fort on a raised mound that was originally an island. The fort was a large circular construction outfitted with embrasures for cannon placement for mock battles, enjoyed not only by children but also, it was reported, on house-party weekends when a dozen men retreated here and the distaff guests rowed up in boats with silver prows to pelt them with oranges from Aime's grove. Now the fort is reduced to a fragment of wall and base, revealing a stone construction dotted with bits of coral as it struggles to withstand the encroachment of vines and new trees.

Just across the streambed from the fort is a larger unnatural mound—Eliza Ripley's mountain, which was a creative re-use of earth dug out to create the riviere. Within the mound, once capped by a pagoda, was an ice house. It also held the grotto where Valcour Aime spent his days alone in prayer after the death of his son.

A visitor to the garden in the late nineteenth century saw the manmade mountain still carpeted with flowers that edged a path winding from bottom to top. Now bits of brick, rock, and stone peep out between leaf mulch and underbrush over its flanks, making the mound look much too unstable to climb for a view from the top. Instead, I duck into the moss-lined arched entry and peer in. Its sturdy brick walls and arched ceiling recede into blackness, but I've seen photos from the 1940s; I know that the passageway leads to Valcour Aime's grotto with its vaulted ceiling and a small niche that might have held a religious statue.

Beyond the grotto a mammoth pine tree has crashed near the bank of the riviere, flattening a stand of younger trees. It is one of the few trees on the property large enough to have possibly dated to the founding of the garden, and the girth of the pine's trunk makes me wonder if it might have felt the steps of Valcour Aime. The same thought occurs again as we step over a gnarly vine, its circumference as large as a man's fist, that crosses the stream bed and wraps authoritatively around trees on both banks.

Within a short distance, the other side of the riviere's loop joins to form a single streambed leading to a pond that was situated just in front of Aime's elegant mansion. Now the pond is only a depression, puddled with last week's rain, with a circular brick foundation at its center, the base of a long-missing fountain. Crowded in by the wild forest, it is hard to imagine this pond once reflecting the façade of the majestic, grandly columned house.

To locate the cascading waterfall fountain, the last feature on Scott's tour, we must climb out of the channel and bushwhack once again through the overgrowth. The brick and rock structure had been constructed to Valcour Aime's liking so that water spilled over the top, splashing down across its uneven surface to make interesting designs and pleasant sounds. But the waterfall, like everything else, is greatly deteriorated. A piece of its front wall can be seen beneath the vines, ferns, and small trees that have rooted in its crevices but its back wall is too overgrown to approach.

I follow Scott, fighting through the overgrowth toward the little entrance gate, and we soon pass from this wild setting with its decaying relics into an open landscape—a road, cane fields, a high school, contemporary houses. And I think I understand why it is fitting to leave Valcour Aime's unique and extravagant garden standing as a protected island of wild overgrowth. Despite the ravages of nature and man over a century and half, this property still bearing Aime's imprint is honored best as its present owners allow it to slowly disappear in its own way.

5

The Story of Those Columns

From the River Road, passersby may never notice the mysterious stand of architectural stubs in the shadows of a grove of old oaks. The site is almost lost within the surrounding sweep of pasture dotted with grazing cattle; no clue to the identity of the weathered ruins remains.

For almost a century and a half, everyone knew this place as The Cottage Plantation. She was an elegant antebellum mansion that reigned like a queen over the sharp elbow of land known as Conrad Point just south of Baton Rouge. The house arguably claimed the most dramatic setting of any plantation along the River Road, nestled in a dense grove of oaks, magnolias, and pecan trees and situated on the point to take advantage of the glorious sweep of Mississippi River, which wrapped around the property. Visitors always exclaimed over the dramatic view.

But in 1960, a swift and raging fire reduced the handsome house to rubble in a matter of hours. Only the prominent verticals of brick chimneys and columns finally remained, most often referred to as "romantic ruins" as they were allowed to slowly disintegrate through the years.

I'd always noticed this architectural anachronism sitting starkly among the grassland and complacent cows and was curious about its story. And, as I poked about the rubble in the company of one of the current owners, I thought I could still sense a palpable sense of loss.

My escort had been a teen when the fire destroyed The Cottage; she is among the last generation of Conrad descendants who enjoyed the old country house, felt its charm.

The river still makes its broad run around Conrad Point, but the crumbled and weather-beaten remains of The Cottage have long been protected by a fence surrounding the property that is adorned with no-nonsense "No Trespassing" signs. They were erected because treasure hunters once assumed that something of value must be left in the vestiges, and lovers were enticed by some indescribable aura. Today, there is nothing of value to be found and no privacy for lovers amid the scattered brick remains grown over with dandelions and blackberry vines and rosettes of cabbage thistle.

Soon after the dramatic fire, one of owners of The Cottage was asked about the family's plans to rebuild. "It could be rebuilt," she replied thoughtfully, "but never replaced because of its history." But, she might have added, I hope it will never be forgotten.

First, the name: a bit of mistaken identity. In the early nineteenth century, New Orleans attorney Abner Duncan bought various tracts of land on the prominent Mississippi River point and consolidated them into a single large property located on what was subsequently identified as Duncan Point. He built a modest home where the family retreated for vacations, saying they were "going to the cottage." In 1824 when Duncan's daughter, Frances, married Frederick Conrad, Duncan's young law associate from Virginia, Abner built for the young couple an elegant house near the family getaway. Somehow the new house also became known as The Cottage, with capital letters.

The proud father spared no expense. The new mansion was constructed in the classical revival style so popular during the period, with slave-made plastered brick on the lower floor and hand-hewn oak and cypress above, all encircled by a broad gallery supported by plastered Doric columns on giant pedestals. The gallery was so broad, in fact, that when the family decided to add an indoor kitchen and other rooms in the 1920s, the back corners of the gallery were simply enclosed without adding square footage. And more than one visitor commented on the front entrance to the house, which featured graceful rounded steps that led to a heavy paneled front door, flanked by fluted columns and handsome sidelights, and topped with an arched fanlight.

The walls of The Cottage were two feet thick. The house contained twenty-two rooms—eleven on each of its two main living floors, each floor divided by a broad hallway. On the ground floor, two large parlors were separated by folding paneled doors that could be opened with a tug on their silver doorknobs into a single large room. Across the hall from the parlors were a library and music room, each finished with mahogany woodwork and Italian marble mantels.

The graceful stairway to the second floor had ornamental mahogany carvings along its treads and a polished mahogany handrail. A small stair continued from the second floor up to the attic, but the attic itself was a grand space with six dormer windows and "intriguing cubby holes and garret hiding places," according to one nosy visitor. From the attic, another narrow stairway led through a trap door onto an observation platform at the level of the gray slate roof, affording the most spectacular view of the property and the river. After Frederick Conrad had become an immensely successful sugar planter, the view also would have encompassed elaborate gardens surrounding the house and, to the rear, a village of brick slave cabins, a large sugar house, an overseer's home, and a myriad of other outbuildings on the property, which had become known as Conrad Point.

The 1860 census lists Frederick Conrad as a farmer who owned 1,400 improved acres and 1,545 unimproved acres, 248 slaves, 50 slave dwellings, and livestock. It reveals a successful man, but it couldn't reflect in bare statistics how important he had become: he was also a state legislator and the host to famous friends such as the Marquis de Lafayette, Zachary Taylor, Judah P. Benjamin, Jefferson Davis, and Henry Clay.

Nor did the census reveal the heroic role that The Cottage had played the previous year in the rescue of passengers from the steamer *Princess*. On February 27, 1859, the *Princess* was en route to New Orleans for Mardi Gras, carrying more than 250 passengers and a load of cotton. She had apparently been pushing her engines hard to compensate for time lost due to fog when her boilers exploded and burst into flame at a place on the river called Red Eye Crossing. She nosed toward the bank just upriver from The Cottage. A slave from the plantation swam out to grab the boat's line as the overseer took charge. Slaves from Conrad's place joined by planters and slaves from nearby plantations pulled survivors from the water and laid them on the broad, shady lawn of The Cottage. The scalded victims were rolled in bed sheets filled with flour, at the time considered the most effective treatment for burns.

James Morris Morgan witnessed this tragedy and wrote about it in his memoir, *Recollections of a Rebel Reefer*. "As fast as the burned and scalded people were pulled out of the river," he remembered, "they were seized by the slaves and, while screaming and shrieking with pain and fright, forcibly thrown down on the sheets and rolled in the flour. The clothes had been burned off of many of them. Some, in their agony, could not lie still, and, with the white sheets wrapped round them, looking like ghosts, they danced a weird hornpipe while filling the air with their screams." Approximately seventy people died at the dreadful scene.

That was drama enough but two years later, when the Civil War broke out, The Cottage came under siege. Before the war, Frederick Conrad, a Confederate loyalist, had argued with a nephew, trying to dissuade the young man from joining the Union navy. The nephew followed his own path and was subsequently assigned to a boat patrolling the Mississippi, so each time he passed Conrad Point, his boat bombarded The Cottage, shelling the house and grounds and sending the family fleeing to shelter behind the levee. Union troops also prowled The Cottage grounds, leading Conrad's daughter-in-law, a pregnant Mrs. Duncan Conrad, to stuff the family jewels in a chamois pouch and hang them around her neck as Federal soldiers stomped through the house looking for valuables.

Despite these intrusions, Frederick Conrad intended to remain in his house throughout the war. The 1862 surrender of nearby Baton Rouge to Union forces, however, changed his mind. The seventy-year-old Frederick and his family joined other residents fleeing the area. The Conrads spent the duration of the war in St. Helena Parish. While they were absent, Federal troops took over the property, converting the house into a hospital for wounded soldiers and victims of yellow fever. For a long time after, locals whispered that a Union graveyard had been dug on The Cottage grounds.

After the war, the family returned to find the property devastated; Frederick died before he could see it restored by his brothers. The mysterious Angus Holt also returned with the family after the war. Holt had served as Frederick's personal secretary, tutor to his children, or head gardener—it was never clear. But after the war, he became wildly eccentric and when he died in 1880, it was rumored that his spirit remained, the ghostly caretaker of The Cottage.

The Conrad brothers oversaw repair of the mansion and outbuildings and replanted their fields but after a decade of diminishing sugar production, they tore down the old mill, converted their crop to cotton, and built a gin. By June 1870, it seemed that life at The Cottage had regained some of its former vitality, as evidenced by a party gathered on the curving levee of Conrad Point to cheer the famous race between the steamboats *Natchez* and *Robert E. Lee.*

Cotton, too, proved challenging because of a devastating infestation of boll weevils. So, in 1917, after The Cottage was used as a set for the filming of the silent movie *Burning the Candle,* the Conrads abandoned Conrad Point. The land was leased to tenant farmers but the beautiful house remained unoccupied for many years, with a resident caretaker to ensure that the mansion would never reach a state of complete dereliction. Although a newspaper article reported that "the exterior took on a weathered look, with cobwebs on every door and window," it was believed that the ghost of Angus Holt protected it from intruders.

Holt's ghost, however, didn't dissuade author Frances Parkinson Keyes from renting the place in 1943. The popular novelist spent two years in residence at The Cottage, writing what became the best-seller she titled *The River Road.* "I went to live [there] in order to acquaint myself with the locality I wished to use as the setting for a novel," Keyes told an interviewer, adding that she already had heard the place was haunted. It did have an eerie quality, she acknowledged, "especially in the moonlight. But that is true also of the great trees, draped with white wisteria and Cherokee roses, as well as waving gray moss."

In *All This Louisiana,* a memoir about her stay in the state, Keyes reported that she had spent almost $50,000 to restore The Cottage during her residency. The book included photographs of the gardens, showing clipped borders surrounding beds of flowers, carefully tended parterre gardens, and a decorative sugar kettle amid a bursting of semitropical plantings. But she complained that the two victory gardens she had planted were ruined—one because of drought and the other because of seepage. This latter condition was an ongoing effect of the river's natural hydrology, caused by the current in high water slamming against the bank on the upriver side of the point. It remains a characteristic of the property even today.

Keyes also complained about the rural nature of her residence and its deficiencies—having to get along "without a telephone, without mail service, without delivery of any commodity, even a newspaper." She was aggravated that water service was cut off intermittently and the roads became impassably muddy. And she was particularly outraged by the wildlife, writing crossly, "I have found everything from snakes to skunks on my doorstep, and I have been obliged to combat mosquitoes and other insects that got past window screens and mosquito bars."

Despite all this, The Cottage somehow won her over because she insisted that a picture of the house be the image on the cover of *The River Road.* "Even in my moments of greatest depression," she confessed later, as if to counter all her bad humor, "I knew down deep in my heart that the beauty of my surroundings, the wealth of my material . . . were far more significant than any obstacle in my path."

After Frances Parkinson Keyes departed, the Conrad descendants reoccupied The Cottage, only to discover that the writer's celebrity had turned it into a popular attraction. Tourists, artists, and photographers appeared at Conrad Point for a view of the house and the environs where the famed novelist had stayed. Family members recalled waking from a nap on a weekend afternoon to find curious strangers peering in from a doorway or through a window. One bold visitor confessed that she'd paid an old man to let her in to look around.

With such attention, it seemed entirely logical for the family to take advantage of their house's popularity and open it to a paying public. In the early 1950s, the family incorporated their ownership of The Cottage into a business and restored the mansion as a showcase. An advertising brochure from the time sets the tone: elegant cream stock printed with a pleasing light gray font with charcoal highlights and a rendering of the colonnaded façade of the house. The brochure explained that the family corporation was dedicated "to preservation and exhibition [of The Cottage] as an historic southern landmark," open weekdays from 9 a.m. to 5 p.m. and Sundays from 1 to 5 p.m., for an admission of ninety cents. A color postcard of The Cottage, dated 1959 and used in a state tourism study of potential attractions along the River Road, shows a handsome white house with dark green shutters encircled by the stalwart colonnade and shaded in the grove of massive old oaks. The brick front walk, lined with masses of low plantings, leads to the front door, still surrounded by the pilastered columns, sidelights, and fanlight that Abner Duncan's architect had designed.

The Cottage remained a popular tourist attraction for visitors until February 18, 1960, when the fatal fire began. Discovered by the caretaker about 3 a.m., it was thought to have been caused by lightning. When a fire truck arrived half an hour later, the wind still whipped flames through the building and the water supply was inadequate to fight the fire. One of the owners, summoned from town, arrived to see "the flames reflected on the low clouds . . . it looked like the mushroom from an atomic explosion except there was no smoke—only light."

He painfully observed that the exquisite architecture of the house "was never more evident than this morning, when [its outlines] could be seen through the curtain of fire, perfect in its symmetry." Another owner ruefully remarked that in recent years, the house had been better cared for while vacant, appreciated as a tourist attraction more than at any time since before the Civil War.

Several days after the fire, a reporter compared the scene to the site of a World War II bombing disaster. Some columns, he wrote, were broken in half, others were ready to topple. The tall brick structures of the eleven fireplaces were undermined and loomed precariously. "The only remains [are] the brick lower story and a few half-toppled columns." It was a terrible sight with "broken bed springs, a blackened hat rack, a half-buried pot-bellied stove, a twisted antique light fixture resting atop the bricks . . . crushed pieces of valuable china filtered through the debris and antique furnishings charred beyond recognition."

Ever since the fatal fire, the ruins of The Cottage have been the subject of occasional newspaper and magazine articles. Accompanying photographs have showed the columns rising from the field and the crumbling bricks of the first-floor walls. As the years have passed, however, the outlines of the old house have grown perceptibly less distinct, the columns slowly diminishing against the landscape.

And so the old house on Conrad Point remains a landmark, steeped in history and lore, even as it slowly disappears.

❧ III ❧
Cultural Collections

6

My Guide at Carville Is Mr. Pete

Some afternoons, Simeon Peterson parks his short, electric-blue bicycle in the covered walkway behind the National Hansen's Disease Museum. He steps inside and removes his black straw fedora, transforming himself into Mr. Pete, docent on duty. He will guide you through the rooms of this unique facility, telling about some of the eclectic assortment of photos, artifacts, and memorabilia that reveal what life was like at the National Hansen's Disease Center, better known for over a century simply by the shorthand of its host community, Carville.

Mr. Pete, a short, squarish man with mahogany skin, has round eyes that twinkle behind large eyeglasses set on a broad face. He shuffles slightly, owing to his eighty-something years, and points out favorite exhibits in a soft voice still inflected with the lilt of his native St. Croix. It's a job he has enjoyed since 2009, and he would seem like any other senior volunteer enjoying a few hours in an interesting place, but his hands give him away.

Most of the fingers on Mr. Pete's hands are gone. On his right hand are only a forefinger and a reconstructed but disfigured thumb; on his left hand, a disfigured thumb remains. Above his knuckles are pointy stubs covered with taut skin, and beneath the short sleeves of his blue-striped shirt, his arms reveal the subtle tracks of painful tendon surgeries, performed years ago to allow him to unfurl the bones in his hands.

Simeon Peterson is a Hansen's Disease patient, one of thousands who have lived at Carville. He has been there since 1951, the longest-residing patient among the handful who remain. This place is his home.

So it is a privilege to follow Mr. Pete through the museum, to explore it with the advantage of his first-hand knowledge. But if he's otherwise engaged, as he sometimes is, the museum is easy enough to meander through independently, easy enough to look at the photos and artifacts and read the texts and labels. Easy enough to get a sense of the horrifying—and heartwarming—story of this singular place, the only facility of its kind in the continental United States.

A visit to the museum is the best way to understand the remarkable story of what happened here—medical failures and triumphs, an unusual way of life, and a community of people: patients, both ordinary and outstanding, heroic doctors and dedicated staff interwoven through a web of love and joy, pain and sorrow.

The museum is crammed with personal belongings of onetime patients: antique wooden wheelchairs and creative Mardi Gras costumes; the re-creation of a patient's room circa 1940; an exhibit that honors the Daughters of Charity, whose dedicated tenure at Carville lasted over a century. An especially poignant photo that expresses the character of life at Carville shows a patients' garden edged with inverted Coca Cola bottles, their sculpted bases making an attractive border around the plantings. But the extensive collection of bottles had only accumulated because the company was too fearful of accepting returns from "leprous" Carville and refused to take the bottles back. Only later, after rival Pepsi Cola had begun to service Carville's account, did that relationship change.

The museum is not the only destination at Carville; a visit can also include a self-driven circuit through the sprawling green and tree-shaded campus, past some of the important buildings remaining from when Carville bustled with activity related only to Hansen's Disease, when it was world's leading training and research center for an illness dreaded since biblical times.

Visitors like me arrive at the museum every day to try to appreciate what Carville meant. But others, like Gary Hietala and his wife Diane Pollmer, come to Carville for more personal reasons. They wanted to learn about Gary's grandfather, Alexander, a Finnish immigrant to Minnesota in 1913, who worked in the iron mines, purchased a farm, became a successful farmer and family man. But suddenly the trail of his life abruptly disappeared. Alexander wasn't buried in the family cemetery in Minnesota and no one ever discussed what had become of him. It was as if he had vanished, shrouded in the same kind of secrecy, Diane believed, that was usually reserved for relatives who suffered from mental illness.

Soon after Gary's aunt, the last of Alexander's children, had died, a close family friend asked the couple a shocking question: did they know that Alexander had had leprosy and was sent to Carville in the early 1930s?

Their emotional trip to Carville helped complete Alexander's biography. They learned that he had been patient number 1134; he had spoken little English and probably lived an isolated existence at the facility; he always carried a photo of his children (including Gary's father) that had made him cry when he looked at it. They discovered that Alexander had died of heart disease on October 2, 1939, and found his grave in the Carville cemetery. And they spent time wandering about the complex, trying to imagine what this place would have been like for Alexander. After returning home, Gary and Diane erected a stone in the family cemetery; it honored the memory of Grandfather Alexander who, like so many others of his era, had been sent away in shame and secrecy.

Leprosy had been a dreaded disease, perceived as a scourge of humanity for millennia. Its effects when untreated were physically debilitating and horrible to see, including deformities, bone infections, blindness, and paralysis on the skin or in victims' extremities, nerves, and eyes. Patients' faces were contorted with rough and hideous growths; their hands and feet were gnarled. Leprosy, in short, came to be considered such a stigma that the word "leper," actually defining someone with the disease, became a generic term for any social outcast. Only much later was the disease renamed to honor the Norwegian physician Gerhard Hansen, who had discovered its causative bacillus in 1873, and to counter the disgrace caused by the old name. The transition from using the term "leprosy" to "Hansen's Disease," however, was slow and Carville patients worked tirelessly in the 1930s to help convince the outside world to adopt the preferred designation.

The hospital and its ancillary operations were not supposed to have been located in a remote rural area eighty miles upriver from New Orleans. The physicians at the Tulane Medical Center in New Orleans sought to found a leprosy hospital for treatment and research in the late nineteenth century when they realized how many cases of the disease had been diagnosed in the city. But local residents aggressively fought their efforts. Eventually the doctors were directed to Indian Camp Plantation, a large plantation with a derelict big house and a scattering of outbuildings, which they bought for their hospital. Only much later was it revealed that the Louisiana Leper Home, as it was then called, was allowed there because the Louisiana legislature made the deal under the pretext that the land would be used for an ostrich farm.

Seven patients were sent from New Orleans in the dead of a cold December night in 1894, arriving at Indian Camp by coal barge, as trains and packet boats would not allow passage for leprosy patients. The plantation's former slave cabins became patient housing as they were in better shape than the grand mansion. And although a caring Dr. Isidore Dyer, dean of Tulane's medical school, hoped they were being sent to "a place of refuge, not reproach, a place of treatment and research, not detention," it was a harsh existence, improved only slightly when the Daughters of Charity arrived two years later. The nuns cleaned up the big house to use as administrative offices and for patient services. They remained to care for the patients at Carville until 2005.

In 1917, the U.S. Senate passed an act to establish a national leprosarium in the town of Carville, and the sale of the Louisiana Leper Home to the federal government followed in 1920. The following year, the institution was placed under the authority of the U.S.

Public Health Service, becoming Marine Hospital Number 66, the National Leprosarium. It retained that name until 1986, when it was renamed to honor the Louisiana political leader (now the late) Gillis W. Long.

Under the Public Health Service, conditions at Carville began to improve, although at first the most obvious changes seemed to be to the physical plant. Since Hansen's Disease had always been feared as highly contagious—whether hereditary or passed from an infected person to others—Carville's patients were treated harshly. Many arrived by force and faced spending the rest of their natural lives there (although patients were allowed passes to visit their families). In order to gain release from the institution, a patient must have achieved twelve months of negative tests; registering negative results for ten or eleven months, then registering positive, forced them to begin counting again.

Outgoing mail from Carville was sterilized, marriage between patients was prohibited until 1952, and for many years Carville's adult population was not allowed to vote. Married women who gave birth to children were not allowed to raise them; they were fostered or adopted on the outside. Until the late 1940s, the social stigma of having Hansen's Disease was so painful that most Carville patients adopted pseudonyms to protect the identity of their relatives. "I remember when someone was talking about Edwina Parra," Mr. Pete remembered, "and I said, 'Who's that?'" He had known patient Betty Martin, who wrote her memoir, *Miracle at Carville,* under her Carville pseudonym. The book became a national best-seller in 1950, as readers read in amazement her chronicle about her life, including the complications of falling in love with and marrying a fellow patient. But Mr. Pete had never heard the former New Orleans debutante's real name before.

Improvements to patient care came gradually to Carville, motivated in large part by the tireless efforts of patient activists with the help of sympathizers beyond its fences. Together they fought for better treatment for the more than four hundred adults and children who lived together at the institution at any given time. They continued their battle even after the "miracle" arrived—the discovery of sulfone drug therapy that brought radical change to the treatment of Hansen's Disease and the lives of its patients.

Physicians at Carville pioneered the breakthrough therapy in 1941 using a medication originally developed for tuberculosis patients (for whom it was not successful). Carville patients, desperate for a cure, endured painful intravenous injections and experimental doses of the drug cocktail until an easy-to-take oral version was developed.

The sulfone drug treatment thwarted the devastating symptoms of Hansen's Disease, allowing patients already at Carville to anticipate great improvement and earlier release. Until 1965, however, it remained mandatory that anyone in the continental United States who had been diagnosed with Hansen's Disease must repair to Carville, even if only for a few weeks. After their case was diagnosed and understood, they were released to continue receiving medications and treatment through clinics near their own homes.

At the same time, doctors at Carville also began to realize that the disease that had been feared so reflexively for thousands of years wasn't highly contagious after all. Research revealed that more than 95 percent of the world's population was naturally immune to the bacillus; only the susceptible 5 percent could ever be affected. This explained an apparent second miracle: no staff at Carville—including doctors, medical assistants, workers on the property, or the 108 Daughters of Charity who had iteracted daily with Carville's patients for over a century—had ever caught the disease.

Simeon Peterson was in the unlucky 5 percent. At six years old, he was hospitalized in St. Croix with a mysterious spot on his cheek, eventually diagnosed as Hansen's Disease. He might have spent the rest of his life there without effective treatment but for a woman at the hospital who knew of Carville through the crusading newspaper *The Star*, headed by patient activist Stanley Stein. She recommended his transfer.

Mr. Pete was twenty-three when he arrived at Carville. The nerves in his hands had already been ravaged by the disease "so that when I pick up a hot cup, I don't know it and burn yourself [*sic*]," he explained. "It messed up the joints of all my fingers." His unsalvageable fingers were surgically removed, but the fingers "they curled up into paws and I couldn't use them," which necessitated the tendon surgeries in his arms.

He was assigned to live in Building 31, "the building for colored people," Mr. Pete noted. At the time, the sprawling 350-acre campus was segregated twice—not only by race but also between patients and staff, the separate sides of the compound were marked by a fence in the early years, later by only a hedge. Mr. Pete arrived just as chaulmoogra oil was being replaced by the new sulfone drug therapies. The oil, a medication made from the seeds of a species of tree found in India and China and administered by pill or injection, had been the treatment for leprosy since the 1920s, the best medication available but not highly effective. Mr. Pete considered himself lucky to have arrived when he did, even though injections of sulfone drugs were painful.

Although many patients had been wrenched from their real lives and confined in a place where the community's commanality was only their diagnosis with a dreaded disease, most adjusted to life at Carville. It was racially, culturally, and educationally diverse population contained within a complex of attractive buildings. These were interconnected by two-and-a-half miles of semi-enclosed passageways like the one Mr. Pete still follows to the museum. Today these corridors are quiet, but in the heyday of Carville's history they bustled with the activity of patients riding bicycles or in wheelchairs, or walking to a destination, past doctors, staff members, and nuns, among carts delivering laundry, mail, and meals.

The corridors furnished protection from the weather to the infirmary, the patients' dining hall and its cafeteria-style meals, a complex of two-story dormitory-style buildings with rooms and apartments, and administration buildings. Patients flocked to the popular recreation center with its four-hundred-seat theatre—a venue for plays, movies, and an annual Christmas pageant, a patient canteen, and an upstairs ballroom large enough for the patients' annual Mardi Gras parade, which always included floats and costumes. Walkways connected to the residence of the Daughters of Charity and to separate Catholic and Protestant chapels.

Also within the Carville community was a bank, a post office, barber and beauty shops, a cleaners, a bakery, and a library. There was an accredited school for school-age patients, who were taught by the nuns, and a nine-hole course for golfers. Carville's highly competitive softball team hosted league games on their first-class home field, as the patient-athletes were forbidden to leave the facility to play elsewhere. To the rear of the property, a manmade lake had been dug. Named for long-serving, popular doctor Frederick Johanson, it offered paddleboats, picnic tables, and barbecue grills for patients to enjoy.

Near the lake were a cluster of jerrybuilt buildings, which Betty Martin described as having an atmosphere of independence and secrecy. Here a certain coterie of patients were allowed to gather in what sounded like a mix of fraternity house and salon. Later, married couples moved in. Eventually the Public Health Service replaced the buildings with cozy brick homes. Also dotting Carville's four hundred acres were its dedicated water treatment and power plants, a dairy, extensive gardens, patient and staff laundries, and the cemetery.

Doctors and staff members lived in comfortable frame buildings grouped together at the front of the property near River Road. They shared a dining hall, now the museum building. Their part of the campus was far enough from the famous "hole in the fence" that they could not claim responsibility for patients who, out of sight of the guardhouse, literally slid beneath the security fence. These secret and unofficial escapes into the real world might only be for a mile-and-a-half walk down the road to the Red Rooster Bar, or it might be into a taxi for a surreptitious visit to the bright lights of New Orleans or a football game in Baton Rouge.

Every able patient at Carville had a job or a volunteer position. Some worked at *The Star* newspaper; others were secretaries, visitor guides, medical assistants, dishwashers, and the like. Mr. Pete relished his responsibility as hospital elevator operator, for which he remembered being paid the rate of sixty cents an hour. He commanded his carrier from the first floor, just for women, to the second floor, just for men, up to the third-floor deck, where patients in wheelchairs could go outside. "It was so nice, cool, and quiet," he remembered, confessing that he wasn't supposed to go out there. "Sometimes I'd walk out [to enjoy the view] and then patients would ring and ring the elevator button, get mad when I made them wait." His broad face broke into an impish grin at the memory.

The Carville calendar was filled with celebrations, according to Mr. Pete—festivities such as Mardi Gras and the Fourth of July, as well as an annual May event when "we'd have the American Legion fish fry and beer on the lake," one of his personal favorites. Some patients hosted private parties in their residential areas, and everyone but Simeon Peterson seems to have decorated their living spaces for Christmas.

Life at Carville began to change in the 1980s after the hospital no longer accepted residential patients. Then, in 1999, the federal government returned the title to Indian Camp Plantation to the state of Louisiana. Thereafter, anyone diagnosed with Hansen's Disease would not go to Carville. One hundred and five years after the first leprosy patients arrived at the old plantation on the river, the sprawling, shaded campus hosted an institutional home run by the Louisiana National Guard for young men with behavioral problems.

At the time, 150 Hansen's Disease patients were still in residence and they were given three options, Mr. Pete remembered. Ambulatory patients who wished to stay were allowed, "like in a retirement community"; very ill patients were transferred to a U.S. Public Health Service assisted-living facility in Baton Rouge; the remainder, "mostly younger patients who could take care of themselves and work on the outside," were allotted money to help cover their medical expenses and left Carville to pursue normal lives.

The longest-residing patient at Carville considered accepting the money and moving back to St. Croix. Over the years, he'd gone home a few times to visit his mother and sister "but people there saw my arms and hands and asked if I'd got burned." He looked saddened, then confessed, "I say yes because if I tell them I'm in Carville with Hansen's Disease they don't know what it is. And if I say 'leprosy,' they would run." Since his last visit home, however, both his mother and sister have died; his only living relatives are a niece and her family. "But I really don't know them," Mr. Pete admitted, adding with a wry smile, "I don't want to go there and have them ask about Uncle Simeon's hands."

His old friends at Carville are gone—some moved away, others are buried in the cemetery. But he had no regrets about staying. This is his home, where he lives with the few other remaining patients in a single building. We get everything we need, he told me, including food, housing, and medical care, provided free of charge. He keeps busy riding his bicycle around the grounds and going out with fellow patients to a restaurant every week or so. He watches television and, of course, he has his volunteer job at the museum.

The last activity is especially gratifying because it gives Simeon Peterson the opportunity to tell his story and the story of Carville. "I tell people, 'Don't be scared of Hansen's Disease.'" And when he talks to school groups or other children, his message is very direct. "I'd say," Mr. Pete told me with a thoughtful look, "that we're just like anybody else."

It is part of what every visitor will have learned after spending some time at the museum, whether or not they had the pleasure of Mr. Pete's company.

Once upon a Time in St. James Parish

I arrived one day at the St. James Parish Historical Society Museum as two buses of second-graders spilled out onto the tight grounds of the museum complex. The children, buzzing with anticipation, had been studying pioneer life, and each year their social studies teacher made an appointment to bring them from New Orleans to the little museum in Lutcher. Here they had an interactive experience with some of the old ways of doing things in south Louisiana—with River Road pioneering, so to speak.

The tumbling flock of eight-year-olds were divided into groups to ride a short rail on an authentic lumber industry handcart, pumping the handles to propel themselves; to wrestle with the stiff iron wheel of a grinder for the reward of transforming corn kernels into coarse, fresh cornmeal; and to watch as a blacksmith demonstrated how a red-hot poker right off the coals could pierce a hole through a wooden board as cleanly as any power drill.

All this and more dazzled the students, and I—a city gal—enjoyed each demonstration as well. But I'd come to expect such experiences each time I'd visited this crowded, distinctly low-tech jumble of collections that reveals a way of life not only unfamiliar to me but also fast disappearing from St. James Parish. I equate the ambiance of the museum to a grandmother's attic, if grandmother lived in river

Cajun country and had collected and preserved family belongings since the first relatives arrived from Acadia in the mid-eighteenth century. And especially if she was proud of her family history and wanted everyone to understand it.

On a previous visit to the museum, I'd encountered a hearty, white-haired woman in her late seventies giving two Texas families a tour through the complex. They were in the back shed, and the Texans were puzzling over a large bale of black wiry fibers: they couldn't identify the ginned Spanish moss, although they'd just admired its curly grey tendrils swaying from the boughs of old oaks in Audubon Park in New Orleans. They were fascinated to learn that St. James Parish had had a thriving moss-ginning industry—men patrolling the swamps in pirogues, pulling moss from the trees, then cleaning, curing, and selling the product. It was used, the guide told them, for building insulation, packing material, seat padding in some vintage cars, and her favorite—as mattress stuffing. Their "pioneer" guide proudly proclaimed her roots as the Texans warily patted a moss-stuffed mattress. "Yep," she grinned, "I grew up sleeping on this stuff. After nine months, it got so flat that we had to wash it. Then we were happy because we were lying way high again."

Beyond the open door of the moss shed, a large barrel cistern stood high on a sturdy brick base. The cistern's banded cypress slats showed daylight; they were shrunken from too many years as a display without holding water. That was her family's water supply when she grew up, the guide told her visitors: "We didn't have running water." A cistern like this one—but air-tight, of course—captured the rainfall, and then "we just went out with the bucket and put it under the spout." She looked at the children and grinned. "No such thing as hot and cold."

When one of the children questioned the use of a lantern and several other unfamiliar home furnishings in the main exhibit building, their docent confessed that "when I was married in 1949, we didn't have electricity." Lanterns, wood stoves, and grinders that required muscle power were what everyone had to use.

To the Texas visitors and the second-graders, references to an almost unimaginable way of life might well have sounded like fantasy, or certainly pioneering. But even younger residents of St. James Parish, many of whose ancestors lived this way, have the same reactions. That is why the St. James Historical Society Museum was begun.

In 1987, a group of locals began to realize that the unique culture in which they had grown up was disappearing. The familiar traditions and local industries that had defined St. James Parish for a century needed to be recognized and documented before they were completely destroyed or became homogenized beyond recognition.

Two dozen or so longtime residents, as Charlie Duhe recalled, began to gather in each other's homes, reminiscing about the old culture and detailing among themselves how things used to be. This led to forming themselves into a historical society and, not long after, to a decision that they should collect artifacts that told the stories of this vanishing culture. "We looked around to find articles and people who knew things," Duhe told me. The society members were a core, representing generations still around who had known the old way of life. Today, after many of them have died, Duhe and historical society president-for-life Joe Samrow are among the few society founders still involved.

As the group collected artifacts, it became apparent that they would need a dedicated space in which to store them. The dilemma was solved when the owner of the old College Point Pharmacy in Convent offered to donate his nineteenth-century cypress cottage. Then the town of Lutcher made a deal for a piece of land on which to move the building: for $1 a year, the society could have an empty corner lot on River Road, next door to the city's water treatment plant and in the shade of its looming water tower. As with almost all of its subsequent museum projects, society members moved and renovated the building, installing a new floor and roof and adding bathroom facilities. It was the first of their innumerable projects accomplished with their sweat equity and acquired talents, such as knowing how to drag an 800-year-old sinker cypress log from the bottom of a bayou or how to build a brick blacksmith shop from a sketch.

The question that every museum must answer is what its scope and collection will be. "We thought about, 'What's the parish famous for?'" Charlie Duhe remembered. The list began. "The cypress industry, one, so we started with the sawmill stuff." (The town of Lutcher was named for the Lutcher and Moore Cypress Lumber Company, which operated during the golden age of lumbering, harvesting local virgin cypress from the 1880s until the 1920s.) Also definitive in local history: sugar, perique tobacco, moss ginning, trapping, and how people lived day by day.

As friends and neighbors around the parish learned what the society was doing, donations began to arrive. From cupboards, attics, and barns came old furnishings and implements, vintage documents, scrapbooks and yellowed clippings, and an assortment of memorabilia. Organizing the contributions—and the occasional essential purchases—seemed to fall into place organically, though informally. This museum has never been subject to professional curatorial services, the intricacies of gallery layout or lighting, or an analysis of visitor flow. Instead it evolved into an authentic, if offbeat, place, lovingly built, outfitted, and organized through the passion and innate common sense of its members.

Eventually, the society applied for recognition as a nonprofit to qualify for accepting tax-deductible contributions and small grants used to buy construction materials or to purchase antiques from people who wouldn't donate outright. Sometime during this process, the society created a motto for their museum: "History preserved through knowledge shared." This ideal has served to define its mission and purpose and act as the virtual glue binding together the eclectic collection.

The first artifacts were housed in the old pharmacy building, displayed in its original wood and glass cases and rows of shelving. It is still the main exhibit building, with historic local industries—lumbering, sugar, perique tobacco, and trapping—presented through yellowing photos and much-used old implements. The building is also crammed with a sampling of Acadian household utensils, textiles and furnishings, old pharmacy bottles, even found objects from the prehistoric Native American Belmont mound. One wall is covered with black-and-white photographs of antebellum mansions, vintage houses, churches, schools, and stores, many of which no longer exist, as if pulled from a catalogue of St. James real-estate history.

On the museum's compact grounds are assorted structures and heritage objects: the dollhouse-sized Paulina post office, still outfitted for business; an early twentieth-century shoe repair shop in an Acadian cottage; a diorama of the Lutcher and Moore Lumber Company; and the old hand-pumped cart. An 800-year-old behemoth sinker cypress log lies across the front yard, next to a diminutive locomotive engine that once pulled narrow-gauge sugarcane trains. The old cypress cistern looms near the perique tobacco shed, which they built "just like a real shed," Charlie Duhe bragged. It qualifies as the only place in the world that tells the story of a product unique to St. James Parish. Near the Spanish moss exhibit, the fur trapping display offers careful labels for each special stretching board and the tools required to transform native animals into usable pelts. The blacksmith shop is a riot of metal tools hanging from rafters and covering tabletops. One of my favorites was an implement that looks like a waffle iron, but the inside of its cooking plates are decorated with ecclesiastical symbols. This was the press used by nineteenth-century nuns at the nearby convent to make handmade communion hosts for priests to serve at Mass.

For many years, the museum welcomed visitors during regular business hours; there was no need for an appointment because the pharmacy building also housed the parish tourism office and its full-time employee. Historical society members volunteered on weekends and as their real jobs permitted, serving as guides and continuing to add new buildings and exhibits and improve the old ones. "All our labor was free and we all worked," said Charlie Duhe with pride.

But one of the first considerations of an organization is sustainability: how will it survive—thrive—after its founders and original members are no longer in charge? This was a challenge that the historical society hadn't addressed before they began to lose many of their most active members. Those who built and arranged and repaired, collected and volunteered became ill; they died; their surviving peers aged, becoming less able to care for their museum. For some reason the next generation was hesitant to take over. Were they unwelcome by the old guard, or simply disinterested?

The St. James Historical Society might have continued through inertia, but it was forced to face its future when the parish tourism office relocated to a new visitor center several miles away, leaving only society members and other volunteers to run the museum. It began to open only by appointment, when Charlie Duhe, Joe Samrow, or another member was available. The donation jar next to the guest-book at the front door was almost empty, and paid memberships in the society were dramatically reduced. Grant-writing had become increasingly difficult. The museum clearly needed new blood, some organization, and a way to maintain its ability to collect artifacts. As members pondered their options, another unexpected bit of bad news arrived: the town of Lutcher needed to expand its water treatment facility, requiring the museum to vacate its lot.

For a while it looked as if I would write the epitaph of the St. James Historical Society Museum rather than celebrate its story.

And then, quite unexpectedly, the fate of the museum began to change. New leadership within the St. James Parish government seemed to realize that the parish's only museum was an asset, a treasure that could never be duplicated, and an authentic attraction—the kind that tourists seek and locals can be proud of. So the parish issued an invitation: would the museum relocate onto property adjacent to its new visitor center? The parish would assist with moving "lock, stock, and barrel" the buildings, exhibits, and artifacts; the "new" museum would be accessible to the public on a regular schedule. And members of the historical society and old-timers would be welcomed to participate, to tell their stories.

"I would have loved to stay right here on the River Road," Joe Samrow told me wistfully when he related the offer. These changes would redefine the role of the society and their control of the museum, perhaps even alter the museum itself. And the spirit of the museum would certainly change, leaving the unique atmosphere that had been created on that crowded corner lot of the River Road over a quarter of a century.

But Joe Samrow, Charlie Duhe, and the others who care about this museum are inherently wise and uncommonly sensible. Ultimately, they agreed; they wanted most to save the project in which they and so many others had invested themselves. These new circumstances would allow the museum to continue to be available to people like me and the Texas visitors and the second-grade classes from New Orleans. It might even attract the younger generation of St. James Parish, who could marvel at the lives of their own forbears—those pioneers who used cisterns to furnish their running water and slept on mattresses plumped with ginned moss.

All in all, then, this story has a happy ending. The dedicated troupe of volunteers who followed their hearts will have left a formidable and enduring legacy, and history will have been preserved through knowledge shared in the forseeable future.

❧ **IV** ❧

Boats and the River

8

With an Eye on the Batture

One chilly November afternoon almost forty years ago, I was introduced to the Mississippi River batture. A family friend lured my husband and me and our three young children with an invitation for a great adventure over the levee. Like most people who live along the lower Mississippi, I have always regarded the levee as an immutable part of my life and have felt grateful for the Corps of Engineers, which conscientiously maintains it, allowing us to live without perpetual fear of flooding.

Until that adventure, however, I had neglected to notice the batture, that sometimes broad, sometimes narrow, found-land that exists between the inside toe of the levee berm and wherever the water of the Mississippi happens to be. Locals pronounce the word "batcher," almost rhyming with "catcher," but its etymology is more aristocratic: it is attributed to the French verb *battre,* "to beat," making it "the land beaten by the movement of the river." It exists because of the levee.

In the years since that first outing, I have continued to regard the levee as a dependable and worthy ally, but I've come to think of the batture as a quirky but appealing friend.

Although the batture is physically close to the civilized world in many places, it is also removed, because it is invisible from the land side of the levee. Even from the top of the levee, a view toward the river is often rewarded with a sprawl of what seems to be wasteland, of little value except in those areas that have been civilized with a loading dock, a pipe terminal, or a commercial building on stilts. Birders sometimes take an interest in the batture from their perch on the crest of the levee, aiming binoculars at the treetops and shrubbery toward the river, because a variety of avian species follow the Mississippi flyway land in the batture. Depending on the season, my birder friends have claimed to have added Mississippi kites, red-headed woodpeckers, wild turkey, indigo buntings, warbling vireo, and a myriad of other species to their life lists.

But the birds come here because these are natural areas, governed only by the movement of the river that sprawls toward and recedes from the levee. This gives the batture the appeal of a wilderness park or preserve but without a name or formalized identity.

To naturalists, a batture does have an identity: they call it a unique mini-habitat defined by the containment of the levee, a natural community and eco-region. Seventeenth-century French naval officer Jean Bernard Bossu saw it as such, defined by the natural levee and having "a dense woods, deer, bears, and wild buffalo cows with their calves."

Although buffalo have long been extinct in Louisiana, a variety of plants and animals can exist on any particular stretch of batture depending on the season, the location, and water conditions. It also depends on whether the manmade levee was built close to the river's edge or farther back from it. Narrow battures are most easily inundated and may host only a scrim of willows and cottonwoods. But broad swathes of batture can seem as untamed as when the first explorers arrived. They may remain dry for much of the year and host a forest of willows and cottonwoods, plus green ash and sycamore, even the occasional red mulberry, pecan or bald cypress, all tangled with a wild understory of shrubs and vines. Plentiful animals have sheltered in these areas: deer, rabbit, raccoons, possums, squirrels, even an occasional fox. And in the borrow pits (the dirt quarries dug in the batture to furnish levee-building material), pools of retained water hold minnows, tadpoles, and turtles.

It was this "land of discovery" feeling, a wilderness without the bears and buffalo, that made our first batture outing so memorable. Within five minutes of slamming the car doors we passed from manicured spaces and city rituals over the levee into a tangle stretching across a wide flat to the river. It seemed completely removed from the world, as if, in that time before cell phones, we had abandoned all worldly distractions.

We strode through the underbrush, picking our way carefully through the thick trailing vines and clambering over massive tree trunks, some washed clean of bark and as sleek as tabletops. Our leader claimed he knew of the brick remains of an old cistern and some distinctive ridges of old levees, both from plantations claimed by the river generations ago. So we began to search for them but found instead a rusted battery as large as a picnic table and a giant serpent of frayed rope coiled across the silt. A loop of rope and chain strung by a previous visitor hung enticingly from a sturdy tree limb, so we all took a turn swinging. Then we skirted the edge of a long borrow pit and stopped to watch skittering bugs etch the surface of the water with kaleidoscopic patterns.

As we headed toward the bank we encountered a trove of treasures—sections of giant cables and ornately carved driftwood, a neatly built fire ring with ashes from illegal campfires, even the huge metal carcass of an abandoned barge. Trash and debris littered the sand, offering clues to the lives of unknown people living somewhere upstream.

Part of the riverbank was reinforced with substantial chunks of grey rock (called riprap) that the Corps of Engineers had artfully laid down to counter erosion from the muscular forces of river current and boat wakes. We had just arrived at the water's edge when a large tug passed nearby, its churned wake slapping brown water hard against the immovable rock, which deflected it with ripples that made the driftwood dance.

The tug was the first in an intermittent parade of boats that passed at eye level, making us feel at once part of the river scene and very insignificant. From the batture, tugs and tows loomed larger and more commanding than they had always seemed from the top of the levee, and the noises—the I-mean-business rumble and growl of motors and the clanking of marine chains and boat metal—were more immediate.

We sat together on a couple of logs that had beached conveniently like stadium seats and played riverside games of the leader's invention. We tossed chunks of smooth, tan driftwood into the current to race like the legendary *Natchez* and *Robert E. Lee* steamboats, cheering for our favorites. Driftwood was plentiful, offering a limitless game, but when the children grew bored, we switched to target practice. As sizable debris swirled past on the river current, we each aimed and threw driftwood and pebbles at them, giving handicaps for smaller, faster objects and extra points for accuracy. Finally, we just sat there, three adults with three children, escapees from the city, watching birds sail overhead and the brown water rush by, until the angle of the sun signaled that it was time to return to our real world.

I've cared about the batture ever since, although I've rarely mentioned it in polite company, assuming batture lovers an uncommon cohort. So I was delighted several years ago to find *Down on the Batture,* a book written by Oliver Houck, a New Orleans law professor. Through the years he had often explored the batture, a short walk from his home, collecting stories from his experiences. The batture had become a part of his life, a place he enjoyed as if it were his own property. Which he knew it was not.

That is because, unless otherwise specified, the specialty laws that have evolved to govern battures hold that it is private property, owned by "the adjacent landowner," meaning the person or entity holding title to the property on the land side of the levee. Not surprisingly, because batture land is so unstable, this has provided a source of legal argument ever since French colonial settlement. Batture was deemed public property until 1807, when New Orleans real estate developer Jean Gravier claimed that the batture adjoining his land was private. Gravier won in a landmark case in the local court, but Governor W. C. C. Claiborne appealed to President Thomas Jefferson, who declared the accreted land public. The case was finally settled with a compromise in 1820, but subsequent decisions have placed the batture squarely in the private domain. Usually.

The definition of a batture and its use remains complicated because of the salad of jurisdictions that oversee it. These include the Corps of Engineers, the Environmental Protection Agency, the Coast Guard, the U.S. Fish and Wildlife Service, and the Louisiana Departments of Environmental Quality, Wildlife and Fisheries, and Transportation and Development, as well as local governments, zoning and levee boards, and other entities. For example, the state owns the river bottom from wherever low water stands into the river, so any construction over the levee and on the batture entails a state lease. But it also requires permission from the Corps of Engineers. Then, too, anyone is allowed " limited access" to the batture if entering from the river; in that case it is considered public, but only in a qualified way for a certain number of hours. Needless to say, such complex terminology has continued to make real-estate transactions and development on batture lands its own legal universe.

My forays onto the batture have been much less frequent than Houck's and limited to sections where I know access is granted. But often when I travel along the River Road, I succumb to the temptation to climb an accessible levee just to see what the undeveloped batture looks like: is it as broad as a pasture or as narrow as an alleyway? Overgrown or open? But I know better than to wander uninvited into a posted area or onto a commercially developed site.

I hadn't realized how much I cared about the batture in general until a recent spring flood stole it completely away. Historically, spring and early summer high water brings the Mississippi to sprawl across the batture; in some years it slaps only halfway toward the levee, leaving parcels of dry ground. But during the wild spring flood of 2011, a record wash coursed down the Mississippi, raging across the widest batture and climbing the inside of levees to within inches of its crown. The brown water erased all but the tops of the tallest trees and structures, which remained exposed to bravely signal the previous existence of something besides swirling water.

I stood on the top of the levee with the river rushing inches below my boots and looked at the batture I knew best. It was gone, and I felt a loss that I thought might be similar to what people who live in snowy places experience when a cold white blanket of snow hides everything familiar. Finally, the first crocus of spring pushes up to herald the return of the earth. Which was what inevitably happened on the batture. Little by little, the river receded and the land form reappeared. A dirt road that slid down the inside of the levee was revealed, slightly less distinct than before, and the whole form of trees gradually reemerged. When the water pulled away, borrow pits became discrete ponds again, gleaming in the sunshine, and the dense shrubbery again rustled in the breeze, but still leaning slightly downstream from the influence of the mighty current.

Once upon a time, people lived along these no-man's lands on both sides of the river between New Orleans and Baton Rouge. For over a century, independence and poverty as much as a love of intimate river views attracted locals to a life on the batture. Mark Twain saw no romance in the scene, describing battures as "muddy, snake-thick, jammed with driftwood (including entire tree trunks)" and the people who lived there "jeans-clad, chills-racked, yellow-faced male miserable, [spitting tobacco juice] through lost teeth while their raggedy women and children clung to rickety rafts roped to the bank."

After the Civil War, many people occupied jerrybuilt camps balanced on stilts as well as rickety rafts. They were called squatters and trespassers but eventually came to be known more poetically as "batture dwellers." Many of the ramshackle properties stayed in a family for generations, remaining off the grid, beyond property taxes and garbage pickup, even as urban development crowded the levee. Even in rural areas, the battures of many plantations were inhabited by these free spirits. When novelist Frances Parkinson Keyes came from Virginia in the late 1940s to rent The Cottage Plantation south of Baton Rouge, she was alarmed to discover people living on the river side of "her" levee. "They take their chances of being rudely dispossessed, either by the rightful owners or by the river," she marveled. "They live in everything from packing boxes to houseboats and earn a precarious livelihood by fishing, hunting, and the sale of driftwood."

Batture dwellers were usually benignly neglected until the early 1950s, when the Corps of Engineers succeeded in having them all evicted under a mandate to expand and repair the levees. Residence on the batture has been outlawed ever since, except for a single cluster of a dozen or so camps over the levee in uptown New Orleans that was somehow grandfathered in. They are still called camps, although several have been renovated to near-elegance and claim a sweep of Mississippi River as their front yard.

Several years ago, the development of a community park was considered for the batture in downtown Baton Rouge. It would have served as an outdoor museum of the Mississippi River and its hydrology, a place to visit the far side of the levee without fear, with educational and interpretative programming. In high water, visitors would be relegated to the levee top or an elevated viewing pavilion, to appreciate the dynamic of a rising river that had overtaken the batture. Plans for this project, which seemed to be a way to entice people to focus on this unknown area, were never finalized. I was sorry.

And that batture that first charmed me was gentrified in recent years. Now, access ramps connect the River Road to a plaza and benches sit atop the levee. The batture is as open and green as a baseball field, dotted with a few token trees that remain from the wilderness it had been. I've never seen anyone playing on this broad swath of park land or standing at its riverbank, contemplating the river's activity beyond. I did notice, however, that dense and undisturbed wild growth remains at each end of the park. Stands of tall trees, raveled shrubs, and trailing vines still offer something like a wilderness, no doubt still hiding treasures of driftwood and marine debris, and perhaps the remnant bricks of an old cistern.

It remains an "other" world as the Mississippi River continues to roll past.

9

Le Pelican't

Beyond the decorative wrought iron benches and lamp posts that re-development brought to the levee top in downtown Donaldsonville lies a broad flat swathe of batture. Just beyond its ragged edge, a sea-green buoy bobs on the current. Near it, a chunk of dark wood noses above the water, looking like so many of the timbers that ride the Mississippi downstream and get hung up underwater.

But this wooden relic is different: this is the only visible remains of the shipwreck of the seventeenth century–reproduction French warship *Le Pelican,* and the green buoy is maritime shorthand for "Stay away!"

I know that *Le Pelican* is only one among the many ships mired on the dark floor of the Mississippi, all with tales worth telling. But I'd bet that few can match hers for drama, or for her unfortunate and ig-nominious ending.

I first encountered *Le Pelican* in 1997. I remember the circumstances because it was two years before the tricentennial of Pierre LeMoyne, Sieur d' Iberville's voyage along the Mississippi River, and I was seek-ing a compelling story to write in conjunction with the celebration. I heard that a reproduction of Iberville's warship was moored at a boatyard in a rough industrial neighborhood in New Orleans and, intrigued, made an appointment to see her.

The original *Pelican* was a 44-gun flagship that Iberville commanded on the Hudson Bay during King William's War in 1697. Her eponymous reproduction had been constructed in Montreal in 1992, underwritten by a Canadian businessman for the princely sum of $15 million, to serve as a tourist attraction. And she was a dazzling sight when I found her bumping against the dock at Morrill & Associates on the Harvey Canal amid the drab industrial gray. She was much larger and more dramatic than I'd expected—176 feet from bow to stern and 35 feet amidship, sporting three towering wooden masts that were secured with an authentic-looking webwork of shrouds. Her upper decks were highly varnished and gleamed in the sunlight, and her main deck was impressively decorated with arrangements of thick furled ropes. These, I later learned, were merely props, like much else on *Le Pelican*. This boat didn't—and couldn't—sail; she had arrived in New Orleans resting on the deck of a barge.

I climbed her open double staircase, admiring the ornately carved balustrade that coordinated nicely with the boat's other carved woodwork, all painted a garish red, blue, and gold. She also sported faux stained-glass portholes and decorative gun slits and, on the stern, a blue and white rococo-style cameo carving of Neptune that was embellished with her name and home port: Pelican d'Iberville, Montreal.

I spent a delightful morning at the shipyard envisioning seventeenth-century nautical life and chatting with the laconic refurbishing crew, admiring their work. I had no doubt that *Le Pelican* would become a splendid exhibit, but I never did find a buyer for my story.

By the time I had met *Le Pelican* in New Orleans, she already had a credible resumé. Originally positioned on the St. Lawrence River in Montreal, she had welcomed thousands of visitors on her decks with the able and hospitable assistance of actors dressed in seventeenth-century naval uniforms. But too few people had visited to offset the cost of keeping her fit through the harsh Canadian winters, and after a couple of years her owner had begun to look for a buyer. He focused on tourism organizations in more hospitable climates—especially along the Mississippi River—who might find his charming anachronism a fine attraction.

The market for reproduction seventeenth-century French warships was apparently a bit slow, but in 1995 a New Jersey businessman succumbed to her charms. He barged *Le Pelican* to New Orleans for refurbishment, as he envisioned her future mooring somewhere in Florida. In the meantime, certain New Orleans interests made a fleeting pitch to keep her as an addition to the paddlewheel tour boats that plied the Mississippi River from their dock near the French Quarter.

Either destination would have required additional work because *Le Pelican* had a nautical challenge: she could not float in moving water. She had been originally constructed as a wooden boat, but when she began to rot, the extensive repairs included cladding her hull in a steel shell. This was overlaid with wood veneer to allow her to pretend to observers that she was still a wooden boat. She looked good, but could never be in open water because the force of waves and currents sloshing between these two layers would undermine her construction again.

As the owner waited for the perfect offer, his expenses were mounting, and he moved the boat to another New Orleans boatyard. It was there, in 1999, that the town of Donaldsonville entered *Le Pelican*'s life.

Andrew Capone—Donaldsonville businessman, local historian, and tourism commission member—was also president of the Fort Butler Foundation. This last is dedicated to restoring and popularizing the site of an 1863 Civil War battle that took place on the Mississippi River at Donaldsonville. The tourist commission had been seeking a tall ship to reenact the battle when Capone learned about *Le Pelican,* now resting sadly at the New Orleans dock and on the brink of foreclosure because her owner was in arrears on her docking fees.

Capone, whose passions are intense, somehow convinced the boat's owner to donate her to the nonprofit Fort Butler Foundation.

And to anyone who doubted the rationale of placing a seventeenth-century warship in a Civil War context, he responded with the rhetorical question: "What better place to pay tribute to Iberville than here? He named this place *Lafourche* [French for "fork" of the river] and spent the night here in 1699." (This was historically accurate.) Furthermore, Capone contended, *Le Pelican* would add pizzazz to the town's planned riverfront revitalization, which would include the Fort Butler site, an early twentieth-century river ferry exhibit, and commercial developments in the nearby downtown.

The main disadvantage to this arrangement was that it would obligate the Fort Butler Foundation to assume the boat's overdue docking fees—$5,000 monthly—until she was moved. Optimistically, Capone issued a Fort Butler press release promising that "with God's blessings and the help of all involved, *Le Pelican* will be ready to receive visitors by May 2001."

But nothing about *Le Pelican* was ever quite so simple.

An engineering firm was hired to do a feasibility study and concluded four months later that *Le Pelican*'s wooden sides were "not fully bonded to the steel bottom plate and shallow side plate, [making] the wood side plate not watertight." This would allow "water ingress from waves and the sea." Translation: *Le Pelican* could not be floated in moving water, whether on the Mississippi River or even on Bayou Lafourche.

But the engineers also offered an ingenious solution: they proposed to design and build a permanent mooring for *Le Pelican* in a canal—like a graving dock—that would be cut into the flat broad batture beyond the downtown levee . They would create a cradle in which *Le Pelican* would sit on a framework of steel beams. This would protect her hull from changing water levels and the powerful current of the Mississippi. She would be connected to the (soon to be gentrified) levee by an elevated walkway, providing visitor access even in high water.

The project merely required a bit of time and planning, and considerable funding—about half a million dollars, Capone calculated. Since the Fort Butler Foundation did not have such a sum, Capone and his fellow enthusiasts promptly set out to find underwriting from officials with the city, parish, and state governments. They trumpeted an optimistic economic development report that promised an annual revenue of $2 million and almost two hundred new jobs generated by the project. But none of these entities appreciated the vision of *Le Pelican* reigning over the Donaldsonville riverfront, which left the Fort Butler Foundation saddled with mounting expenses.

What to do? The obvious, though painful, solution was to sell their handsome boat. So the foundation put out inquiries, which, Capone detailed, led to tremors of interest from along the Gulf Coast—Lake Charles, Galveston, and Mobile—and a very promising response from someone in the tiny southeast Louisiana town of Lafitte. "We could have made a profit," Capone said darkly, in hindsight, after the city fathers of Donaldsonville quite suddenly changed their collective mind and decided in May 2002 to make *Le Pelican* part of the new riverfront.

A deal was struck. The Fort Butler Foundation donated the boat to the city, which assumed her $55,000 debt for docking fees and other expenses. A new nonprofit organization, the Sieur d'Iberville Historical Society of Donaldsonville, was created to manage the *Le Pelican* project, and they made plans to move the boat from the expensive dock in New Orleans upriver closer to Donaldsonville, to await completion of her special cradle.

Calvin Ishmael, the owner of a local fleeting company, was awarded the contract to reposition the boat and provide her temporary mooring at a dock in the shadow of the Sunshine Bridge, several bends downriver from Donaldsonville. In October 2002, *Le Pelican* arrived at her way station and was tied up to mooring dolphins in the river. Apparently, however, she was not properly secured, for in November she began to leak. No one knew why. Ishmael contended that the leak was beyond his control due to "a force majeure," specifically the earthquake in Alaska that created a wave that came up the Mississippi and capsized the boat. And it was true that the Denali fault earthquake on November 3 was the largest inland upheaval in North America for 150 years, causing ripples in pools and lakes as far away as Louisiana and Texas.

But betting men seemed more inclined to believe that inept mooring, exacerbated by bad weather, had been the cause. It seemed as if *Le Pelican* had become grounded on the bottom of the river when the river level began to fall, causing her to settle and list. This had allowed quantities of water and sediment into her hull. On Thanksgiving night, heartbroken members of the Society learned that *Le Pelican* was almost completely underwater; they raced to the river to bail her out.

Soon, however, another equally unnerving discovery came to light. The boat was moored on the property of the Eagle Asphalt Company, a business Ishmael did not own. As she leaned ever more dramatically toward the water, one of her masts threatened to hit the company's floating dock, "so we had to cut it off," lamented August Tassin, who as president of the Sieur d'Iberville Historical Society was now invested in her well-being. *Le Pelican*'s once-gleaming decks were half underwater, her hull filled with sediment. She was a sight.

Now she needed to be salvaged.

Everyone agreed that the salvager awarded the job had to be very familiar with the vagaries of the Mississippi River, a specialty. This easily led to selection of a qualified company that was already working on the Sunshine Bridge with cranes, barges, and other heavy equipment in place. The company agreed to rescue the boat with one stipulation: the river—now rising—could not exceed seventeen feet in depth measured at the bridge for them to proceed. The Society, anxious to have their boat rescued, rushed the contract to the city attorney, but municipal gears ground slowly; in the three weeks it took for the city attorney to certify and the mayor to sign the contract, the river rose above seventeen feet. The contracted company legally withdrew.

The Society, desperate to find another willing salvager, located a company called American Oceanics, based in California. "It was the only player left," Tassin said. The city agreed to a contract with a stipulation of its own: no payment would be made on the project if the ship couldn't be raised.

Meanwhile, a chemical company with a river dock near the sunken *Le Pelican* complained that pieces of the ship—deck doors ripped from the hull by the current, as it turned out—had floated onto their dock. So one of the Society's members rode out in a motorized pirogue to rope the doors and pull them to safety, but he was forced to enlist fellow board members for help: at seven feet long and a foot thick, each door was too large and heavy for one river cowboy to rescue by himself.

American Oceanics rented a house in Donaldsonville for their crew and planted two members in a tent on the batture each night to protect *Le Pelican* and their $250,000 worth of salvage equipment. By July 2003, when the official operation began, the boat had been submerged for nine months.

The first step in salvaging *Le Pelican* was to pump out tons of mud from her hull, which required divers to swim in and position hoses and suction tubes. When the mud had been cleared, they would attach hydraulic pulleys to lift her off the river bottom.

It was at this point that I crossed paths with *Le Pelican* again. I'd hunted up August Tassin, who agreed to take me to see her. He drove to the levee and we walked along a steep shell road over the top through the thick odor of asphalt. It seemed a circuitous route, and I asked why we didn't simply cut through the underbrush on the batture. "Water moccasins," said Tassin succinctly.

From the bank, I could see the boat, still tied to her moorings in the shadow of the monumental bridge. Her buckskin-colored hull was faded and scraped and perforated by gashes and holes; her windows gaped. Remarkably, the still-intact masts and rigging rose with some dignity above her collapsed deck; she looked like a lady of the evening on the morning after. But the Society was pleased: she was afloat once more.

The asphalt company resumed its demand for a $1,000 per month docking fee.

As expenses began to multiply, the Society determined to that *Le Pelican* must move once again. But where? As members began pressuring the engineering firm to expedite the process of obtaining permits and begin construction of her cradle, the city granted permission for *Le Pelican* to be temporarily located just off the batture in downtown Donaldsonville. In February 2004, the *Donaldsonville*

Chief reported that the permits had been acquired and a concrete anchor would be poured in the batture. After curing for twenty-eight days, the project would continue: *Le Pelican* would be attached to a stabilizer, the canal dug, and a slide run from the water, pulling her into her special berth on the batture. Work should be completed in a month, the article predicted with great optimism.

The month passed, and *Le Pelican* was still patiently awaiting her move to the batture and the extensive repairs she required when misfortune struck again: a tugboat slammed into her already fragile body. The tug ruptured its own fuel tanks and spilled diesel into the river but otherwise was unharmed. *Le Pelican,* however, began to sink again, this time quite dramatically, with her bow end submerged, leaving visible only the proud Neptune sculpture on her stern.

The Society was devastated, and the town was in despair. The Coast Guard angrily declared the boat a navigational hazard and demanded that she be moved closer to the batture to prevent her from drifting further into the river's main shipping channel. American Oceanics complied.

The second sinking added millions of dollars to the cost of transforming *Le Pelican* into a viable tourist attraction. But, as luck would have it, she was not insured; after a certain point, she had been deemed uninsurable. Her doors, crossbeams, mast extenders, and other removable parts had already been stored in a local shed, waiting to be restored after she was refurbished. But now city leaders saw little option but to ask the engineers for estimates on the cost of dismantling her, to ascertain how much revenue she might bring as salvage. The longtime chorus of local skeptics resumed their complaints about the boat they called The Albatross and *Le Pelican*'t.

Le Pelican rested undisturbed in her new location until January 2008, when she was hit by a towboat; its crew had apparently not been paying full attention as they changed positions. This accident caused the Coast Guard to shut down a ten-mile stretch of river, disrupting river commerce for almost five hours and bringing more negative attention to Donaldsonville's unique but ill-fated attraction. And that is where she remains today, next to the green buoy floating on its tether, the unmistakable warning to boats and ships to avoid her.

As I've pondered the tale of *Le Pelican,* I began to think it regrettable that another kind of warning wasn't available in the early days to those who loved this boat. Perhaps if I would have found the following information earlier, it might have helped them reconsider their actions.

I learned that her forebear, the original *Pelican* commanded by Iberville, had run aground in 1697 on the shores of Hudson Bay just a few days after the heroic battle. "She'd been badly damaged and suffered further in a subsequent storm," the history reported. "She was doomed. . . . The Pelican's life was short but glorious."

Had the patriarchs of Donaldsonville been the least bit superstitious, such words might have been warning enough.

10

The Queen and I

On a warm June evening in 1977, I leaned across the polished wooden deck rail of the *Mississippi Queen* and waved enthusiastically to no one in particular on a downtown New Orleans wharf. The *MQ*, as the cognoscenti came to call her, was readying to cast off: her calliope brayed notes like a hoarse monster flute; her whistle shrieked and white smoke belched from the lacy filigree atop her black stacks. Then, as the red paddlewheel began to churn the brown water, we were steamboating off toward Vicksburg, just as I'd always dreamed.

I was born much too late for the original steamboat era but, after reading Mark Twain and flipping through picture books, I'd become enamored of steamboats, not so much the packet boats and utilitarian steamboats, but the ornate, wedding-cake-look-alike paddlewheels. I'd admired them in vintage engravings and photographs drifting serenely along the broad river, trailing pennants of smoke, or regally posed at a wharf, expectantly awaiting a journey. They seemed to exude the promise of elegance and adventure, as per Mark Twain's description. "The steamboats were finer than anything on shore," he wrote. "They were indubitably magnificent."

By the 1820s, steamboats had revolutionized commerce on the river, allowing movement of goods upriver as easily as downriver.

(Before steam power, the potent current prevented flatboats and keelboats from traveling south to north.) Mississippi River steamboats had been specifically designed for the vagaries of the river; they sat flat on the water with a shallow draft and often a stern wheel; the fanciest proudly wore a tall superstructure. As Herbert and Edward Quick wrote in their history of Mississippi steamboats, "When the river is low and the sandbars come out for air, the first mate can tap a keg of beer and run the [steam]boat four miles on the suds."

Steamboats ruled the lower Mississippi, the preferred mode of transport for people and commercial goods, until the 1880s when railroads took away much of their business. By the 1930s, steamboats had completely disappeared from the river, reduced to a historic memory.

So I was delighted to learn that a second era of steamboating had arrived: the *Mississippi Queen* was home-ported in New Orleans for part of each year, offering multinight voyages to Vicksburg, Memphis, and beyond—a real steamboat experience as compared to mere harbor excursions on boats with paddlewheels.

The *MQ* had been commissioned a year before our trip, on the occasion of the American Bicentennial celebration when President Gerald Ford saluted her as "a tribute to the heritage of America's inland rivers." She was, at that time, the largest sternwheeler ever afloat, including the most luxurious boats of the original era, and she entered the market with sizzling publicity. (Until the arrival of the *MQ*, in fact, I had never heard about the refurbished, first-generation *Delta Queen,* which already offered overnight cruises.)

The *MQ*'s brochure promised voyages that combined nineteenth-century heritage and steamboat-era nostalgia with the comfort and luxury of a twentieth-century cruise ship. And in complete safety. (It didn't specify the dangers that had routinely beset her nineteenth-century counterparts: explosions, fire, groundings, and wrecks.)

Most of the early steamboats had been utilitarian, dirty, and uncomfortable, more like public transportation than cruise ships, offering only two cabins—one each for male and female passengers. Comfort was not required; in fact, as late as 1917, a packet boat heading to the New Orleans Mardi Gras offered its passengers double-deck bunks in the cabins or cots set up in the dining room and bar, with freight piled up around passengers on the decks. And even the most elegant boats lacked running water until after the Civil War and electric interior lighting did not arrive until the 1890s.

Lovely nineteenth-century steamboats had four decks: an expansive main deck holding cargo, the engine room, and second-class passengers; a boiler-level deck with the kitchen, an office, and staterooms off a long, narrow public room; a Texas deck where more cabins were located (originally for steamboat employees); and a pilot house on top. This configuration led to one cynic describing a steamboat as "an engine on a hull, surrounded by a warehouse and covered over with a hotel."

Steamboats individualized themselves on the river by the shrieks of their whistles, the clang of their bells, and the originality of the decorative cutouts atop their towering smokestacks. The stacks were built disproportionately high so that wood-burning boats would not rain live cinders down on their decks, setting fire to cotton bales, lumber, or passengers. When the first bridges were built across the river (a railroad bridge spanned the channel at Rock Island, Illinois, in 1856), steamboat smokestacks had to be reconfigured—either built shorter or hinged in order to pass under the obstructions. I was charmed by the thought of these alterations, which were no challenge for the *MQ;* her tall decorative stacks could be hydraulically retracted with the push of a button.

I wondered how the *Queen* would compare in luxury to her most elegant predecessors, especially ones like the third-generation *J. M. White.* Although she sailed only from 1878 until she burned and sank in 1886, the *White* was a legend. She was 325 feet long with a public salon large enough, it was said, to hold three-hundred waltzing couples under "seven sixteen-burner gold-gilt chandeliers . . . made of fine brass, highly polished, and then . . . covered with pure gold." Her other decorative accessories included stained-glass skylight windows and gold-plated hardware. Her ample staterooms offered full-size beds and one of her two bridal chambers was paneled in mahogany and satinwood, the other in rosewood and satinwood. All of the *White's* furniture had been specially constructed of heavy walnut with a contrasting inlay of the boat's initials, which were repeated in monograms on her silver service, Irish table linens, and serving pieces.

The *Mississippi Queen* fell a bit short of the *J. M. White* but she offered other amenities. She was longer and taller than the *White,* with five decks, including an observation platform, and her modern conveniences included air conditioning and elevators, the latter for any of the four hundred passengers who preferred to avoid her elegant stairways. Her several public rooms were spacious and decorated with flamboyantly Victorian adornment, but each one afforded breathtaking river views through spotless walls of glass. These huge windows, as well as the endless mahogany railings and brass trims and fittings, were attended by an untiring crew who also kept the deck floors shining at high polish. This team was part of the large group required to keep the *MQ* functioning—mates, deckhands, a master, two pilots, a purser, stewards, engineers, electricians, and a service staff, even a night watchman.

The *Queen's* accommodations, however, were not nearly so splendid as those of the *J. M. White.* Her brochure had described cabins that ranged from windowless interior studios to stateroom suites, so we had chosen a midpriced, centrally located space. But when I unlocked its door for the first time, I was disappointed to see what resembled a sleeper compartment on a passenger train, with stabilized beds, sparse furniture, and a miniature bathroom. (I suspect such accommodations were much improved when the *MQ* was renovated in 1989.) However, the cabin did offer the lagniappe of a tiny private veranda furnished with a small table and chairs, affording our own intimate view of the river whenever we wanted it, a lovely addition.

On early steamboats, passengers could dine, engage in conversations, read, relax, play card games, or gamble. Occasionally, a spontaneous musical or theatrical performance might be presented, compliments of a talented passenger or gregarious crew members. But life aboard these boats sounded almost tranquil. In the waning days of the steamboat era, the *St. Louis Journal,* reviewing a voyage aboard Captain L. V. Cooley's steamboat *America* in 1929, wrote that "the cuisine is excellent. The trip from a passenger standpoint is unequalled for rest and offers the tourist an unusual opportunity for sightseeing."

Like any modern cruise ship, however, life on board the *Mississippi Queen* could be frenetic. Her three bars were open sixteen hours a day and the dining room was large enough to accommodate all four hundred passengers in one seating. Her roster of available activities was extensive: a tiny gym with exercise classes, a movie theater, a sauna and massage area, and a dedicated lounging deck that encircled a pool that resembled a sloshing Jacuzzi. A tiny beauty parlor offered services for hair and nails and a gift shop sold river-themed souvenirs. I resisted them all until, relentlessly pursued by the social director hawking bingo, games, and group parties, I fled into the red-velvet movie theater and lost myself in river-themed films such as *Showboat, Huckleberry Finn,* and *Mississippi,* starring W. C. Fields.

The entertainment I preferred was to be outside on deck, viewing the ever-changing river scene. Once, I opted for the stern deck that overlooked the rolling red paddlewheel, under the whoops of the calliope. The *MQ*'s calliope was the world's largest steam-powered piano and, in a steamboating tradition that dated from 1864, it burst into rollicking melodies at each castoff and landing as well as for occasional concerts. I was intrigued and went to investigate where the notes were coming from: it was a musician seated at a pinched piano keyboard in one of the bars. As he struck the appropriate notes, sounds traveled to the top deck by pipes, where forty-four shiny brass cylinders, encircled by two serene brass mermaids, emitted shots of steam for each pitched hoot.

The bow, however, was the best place for river watching. I spent hours, warm and windblown, watching the ever-changing scene, which was similar in its color and bustle to what it must have always been. In a nineteenth-century description of watching the river from the bridge of a steamboat, Liliane Creté described "A splendid view of the great river confined by the levee." She saw "panoramas on either side of the river—sugarcane fields, forests and sawmills, mansions surrounded by orange trees. The river teemed with activity—steamboats, flatboats, keelboats propelled by long oars, dugouts filled with fruits, vegetables, wild game, etc., going to market in New Orleans."

The *Mississippi Queen* was a party bubble in a sea of commerce but the view was comparable. Although flatboats, keelboats, and dugouts were long retired, the river below Baton Rouge teemed with ocean-going tankers and commercial ships with looming gray hulls and foreign flags, small tugs nudging loads of pipe, gravel, and coal, large tugs hunched behind extended barge trains. Clunky ferries crossed the channel behind us and an occasional small pleasure craft darted in the river like a water bug. Above Baton Rouge, traffic remained heavy but consisted only of tugs and tows, dredge boats, and service craft; ocean-going vessels were purposefully impeded from going further upriver by the construction of an intentionally low bridge.

Life beyond the tall levees was reduced to hints—industries became the tops of geometric metal sculptures; towns were identified by the tops of water towers, church steeples, and the peaks of tall roofs. In some places, the banks of the river was verdant wilderness, mud beaches, hidden corners where Huck Finn might have tucked his raft. In other places, marine commerce had covered the batture with docks and pipes and metal buildings. One morning on a broad sand flat we spied a party, complete with striped canopies, a volleyball game, and a campfire. The partiers hooted and yelled as we passed and the *MQ* bellowed hoarsely in response as we waved enthusiastically. It was like a scene from an old Fellini movie, a colorful moment in unknown time in an unidentified location.

In nineteenth-century steamboating, especially packet travel, riverboats commonly made spontaneous stops. Boats could be flagged down from the bank by waving a torch or a bright cloth to signal the desire for a passenger or cargo pick-up, or even just to give the captain a list of necessities to bring back from a nearby town. When British geologist Sir Charles Lyell visited a River Road Plantation in 1847, he was surprised when the host simply sent a servant out at daybreak to set a signal fire on the levee for a boat to pick him up. Soon enough, a passing steamer appeared through the fog and approached the landing; Lyell was summoned to the dock, his baggage brought on board, and off he steamed to Natchez. Even as late as 1931, the practice was still followed. A Boston newspaper observed that the steamboat *Ouachita* stopped when flagged and didn't even require a wharf. "[She] butts her pug nose into the mud bank, fastens her ropes to a handy tree or logs and swinging her great landing stage as far inshore as it will reach," to welcome a new passenger.

The *Mississippi Queen,* in modern cruise mode, stuck to her fixed itinerary, which included scheduled stops with tours of river towns and antebellum plantations were offered to passengers. And we were amused to inadvertently discover one morning that she was so rigid about her timetable that she had tied up to trees on the bank one night so as to not get ahead of schedule.

Passengers were allowed to visit the *Queen*'s pilothouse at prescribed times, to hear a pilot or captain share his stories of the river. Mr. Winford, the pilot on duty when I climbed to the top deck, had traveled the river for over forty years, studying its bends and points and sandbars. He shared some of the most basic rules that boats on the river had to observe: an upstream vessel yields right of way because it's easier to manage going against the current; a red buoy must be on your right going upstream; a single toot from an approaching boat means that it's going to starboard and a return toot signals agreement; green markers on land signify places that have some river significance even if (to me) they only appeared to be trees and bushes. Mr. Winford alternated six-hour shifts with another pilot, guiding our passage with the aid of a sophisticated console of instruments. After my tour of the pilothouse, I was convinced that the pilot speaking fluent river jargon was the most direct link between our newfangled cruising hotel and the steamboating that Mark Twain knew.

Nights on the river were beautiful. Inside the main public lounge, lights blazed, a combo beat out pop tunes, and passengers drank, danced, and mingled. Outside, the observation deck was quiet, cooled by a warm, moist breeze in a slate-gray night. There were few lights, many stars; it was a world removed from the civilization teeming unseen along the banks. One evening as we watched the river, we saw a point of light ahead that changed to a narrow wedge, then to a wide beam searching. It swung full face and another boat, having rounded a point, headed toward us. A hollow whistle sounded, followed by the *Mississippi Queen*'s answering blast. Soon, on our port, a tug rumbled past pushing a four-barge tow down the river. After it had chugged by, there was just night and the river.

My trip aboard the *MQ* endeared me to steamboating ever after, although I was only on a steamboat on the lower Mississippi one other time, when I was invited to be a speaker on the *Delta Queen*. She was a charming boat but my loyalty lay with the *Mississippi Queen*, my first experience. So I felt as if I'd lost a friend when the *MQ* was pulled from service in 2006 to be overhauled but was instead scrapped and dismantled. Only her 700-pound bell was saved and sent to a steamboat museum in Indiana.

Her sister boats, the *Delta Queen* and the larger *American Queen,* which had been introduced in 1995, also ended their lower Mississippi service. The *Delta Queen* had been operating since 1966 under a waiver from a new law prohibiting wooden-hulled cruise ships from carrying passengers but retired in 2008 to become a floating hotel on the Tennessee River in Chattanooga. The *American Queen* was put into dry dock. I had witnessed the end of the second era of paddle-wheel steamboat voyaging on the lower Mississippi.

In *Life on the Mississippi,* Mark Twain wrote, "At the end of thirty years [Mississippi steamboating] had grown to mighty proportions; and in less than thirty more, it was dead! A strangely short life for so majestic a creature." It was, he wrote, so greatly diminished, its future dimmed.

Steamboating, however, may have become too ingrained in the culture of the Mississippi River to disappear forever because, in 2010, three boat lines announced plans to resurrect overnight river travel on the lower Mississippi. One would be a paddlewheel steamboat: the refurbished *American Queen,* not surprising billed by her new marketing team as "a floating Victorian mansion" and "the only authentic overnight paddlewheel steamboat in America."

I'm thrilled she's back, offering a third, albeit much diminished, era of steamboating, and I predict that it too will prove irresistible to me.

11

The Story of Captain Mike

The sounds of a Mississippi River ferry remain as distinctive and familiar as they were many years ago when I grew up in New Orleans: the metallic clank of the boarding apron as the weight of a car rolls across; the bass thrum of the powerful engines as the ferry sets out into the river; the heavy roar of the engines as they reverse to stop against the far bank. I've heard these sounds and smelled the incense of fuel and river hundreds of times because riding the ferry is one of my favorite outings, allowing me to see the Mississippi from the inside. On a ferry, I feel as if I'm part of the sweep of the history and lore of the great river, despite knowing that ferry rides are brief and the scenery limited.

To most people, ferries were not recreational vehicles but the most practical way to cross a broad stretch of water. Many ferries are, in fact, considered floating roadbeds, linking a numbered highway that runs to the water's edge on one bank to the same numbered highway on the other side. I'm not sure why, but the image of a highway riding back and forth across the river never fails to amuse me.

In recent times, bridges have replaced many ferries along the River Road, leaving only three routes to stitch together the east and west banks. This produced an alarming thought: what if ferries were an endangered species and my long-prized rides might disappear altogether?

I set out to capture the essence of Mississippi River ferries before they became only a memory.

To do this, I determined to hitch a ride in the pilothouse of a ferry, to give me a better understanding of the boats and how they work. Obtaining permission was a challenge, but I was eventually cleared and arrived on the appointed morning at the west bank landing of the Sunshine-Plaquemine ferry, parking and walking past the long line of waiting cars. It was an odd feeling to cross the metal apron onto the deck of the *Lady Alice,* not encased in an automobile onboard a ferry for the first time that I could remember

The morning was bitterly cold and windy. Wintry blasts thrashed the river into whitecaps and made the boughs of the batture willows dance wildly, but the ferry's motor rumbled confidently. A rough-looking deckhand directed me to a hidden metal staircase that climbed to the upper deck and a warm bright room. It had the decor of an industrial office, with white-painted metal walls and ceiling, maroon-painted metal floor and console deck. But instead of Norman Rockwell prints taped to the walls, each side offered an unbroken bank of windows overlooking the river like constantly changing murals.

Captain Mike lounged by the console sipping a mug of coffee. Having read too much Mississippi River lore, I'd anticipated that he would resemble someone from the colorful band of grizzled adventurers Mark Twain described. But Mike was a young-looking thirty-year-old with round cheeks, a pleasant smile, and skin the color of café au lait. A long tattoo ringed the back of his broad neck between his shaved head and the collar of a red velour sweatshirt that hung over the waist of his charcoal trousers. He and his uniform were not quite what I'd expected.

If his appearance was an initial surprise, however, as we shuttled back and forth over the course of the morning, I became more and more admiring of his expertise. Despite his obvious youth, Captain Mike had paid the requisite dues to earn his place at the helm of this bulky craft. I learned that he'd spent twelve years on the water, starting aboard a crew boat in New Orleans, followed by sufficient sea time and command of progressively larger boats to have worked his way up to earning a license for a 1600-ton craft—a Mississippi River ferry. By the time I'd disembarked, I believed Mike was a true descendant of Mark Twain's riverboat men, even though Twain wrote about steamboating, not ferries.

Ferries have played a critical role along the River Road since the first settlements because people and goods needed to cross the river. Ferry services began as small, privately owned skiffs rowed by their owners who charged a fee. After steam-powered craft were introduced, ferries could transport not only people but also vehicles. Sometimes their capacity was limited: a 1919 advertisement for a St. James Parish ferry, for example, boasted its ability to carry two Model Ts on the deck of the family-owned schooner. In a mid-nineteenth-century tariff listing for the Baton Rouge–Port Allen ferry, separate prices were detailed according to the category of who or what was crossing: foot passengers, horse riders, two-wheeled carriages with horse and driver, four-wheeled carriages with two horses and driver, cows and horses, and sheep and pigs. In an oral history interview, Fannie B. Reynaud recalled ferry rides at Baton Rouge in the 1930s. "If cattle were on, you'd wait 'til the next ferry," she remembered, "or you'd drive on and [ride across] surrounded by [mooing] cows."

Passenger-only ferries, called foot ferries, continued to exist after the introduction of the larger, vehicle-carrying ferries. They were rustic craft, even though an advertisement for a St. James Parish passenger ferry service after World War I noted its many improvements, including having upgraded from a skiff. The photograph of the new boat, however, showed something resembling a modern party barge, with an outboard motor, a canopy that skimmed the heads of its standing passengers, and no railings. This was a common construction for pedestrian ferries of the era, and I could imagine the challenge of rocking across the roiling river while standing on the deck with no hand-holds. I suppose that is why photographs also show such craft with their passengers packed in as tightly as an overcrowded elevator. And in one photograph I noticed that the crush of passengers poised to debark down the metal gangway would step not onto the bank but smack into the shallows of the river.

Railroads crossed the river on their own dedicated train ferries, the earliest of which were steamboats with side paddlewheels. Later models were long barges with tracks laid on their decks, which were pushed across the river by tugs. To Fanny Reynaud, they all looked a bit precarious. "When they got the last car on," she recalled, "its back end was always hanging off the ferry."

Ferry services were once important businesses along the River Road and many routes were privately owned, though they were eventually regulated by local or state government agencies. The services were obligated to obtain an official lease and to provide a posted schedule and dependable service. By the 1960s, all River Road ferries had been acquired by either state or local governments, which ran them until bridges forced their closure or they had become too expensive to run.

I had hoped to discuss some of this ferry history with Captain Mike, but it was not relevant. His strict focus was running the boat, and this did not require knowing a historical continuum of ferries on the Mississippi.

Running a ferry requires commanding the symmetrical collection of switches, dials, and controls on the broad console panel. And they almost all come in duplicate so that the captain can sit on either port or starboard, according to which bank he's approaching. There are steering mechanisms, horns, propeller controls (screws), windshield wipers, control transfer levers and other dedicated gizmos, plus a compass, a radar screen splotched with fuzzy green lines (demarking riverbanks, he told me), and a large white ship's wheel. The last, easily the most recognizable from pictures of old-time river boats, is usually just decorative, Captain Mike told me, only used if all of the *Lady Alice*'s hydraulic systems fail.

I noticed that the pilothouse of the *Lady Alice* remained surprisingly quiet; even the noise of the huge engines was only a smooth and steady bass thrum up there, unlike the rattling and powerful roar heard by cars on the deck. As Captain Mike manipulated the controls, however, he awakened a variety of other noises: steamy hisses when he pushed down the control transfer lever; the familiar hoarse, baritone blat of the ferry's horn when he pressed one of the innocent green buttons; tinny gibberish and squawk from his marine and state radios. It sounded like an atonal composition performed by a band of machines.

From the console he could also control the deck lights, call on an intra-boat telephone, and press a button to sound a general alarm, reminding me that dangers still lurk in twenty-first-century river travel. "That's on every Coast Guard–inspected vessel," he assured me offhandedly. "It's for drills, man overboard, and so forth." He folded up a daily newspaper that had been spread across a ledge behind the console and revealed a boldly printed page under a plexiglass frame: *What To Do If a Person Goes Overboard.* But from his nonchalance I assumed that Captain Mike had seldom, if ever, needed to follow the instructions.

On the opposite wall of the pilothouse was a utilitarian desk, filled with an untidy assortment of official papers—time sheets, a master's log of who worked with the captain, who visited the pilothouse (I will be immortalized), and what happened during the day. Reports are also required for weekly fire and rescue drills. Near the desk were a microwave and a small refrigerator, homey touches for the small metal room that serves as his command center, office, and home away from home for eight hours daily on the seven or eight consecutive days he is assigned to duty.

As he readied to cast off, Mike peered carefully at the radar screen, which looked like a green-on-gray, digitally kinetic artwork. "You have to remember what you've seen before so you can know what you're seeing now," he explained, sounding much like Mark Twain's river pilots, although the latter had memorized the changing contours of the length of the river, not a confined area.

I had been perched on a stool, watching cars clank aboard the *Lady Alice*'s metal deck and stop according to the gestures of the deckhands. The boat was built to hold forty-eight automobiles, but because of the size of modern vehicles a run usually holds only forty. This creates a problem at rush hours, when the *Lady Alice* becomes jammed with commuters who live on one side of the river but work on the other. Many times between five o'clock and seven-thirty in the mornings and during late afternoons, more cars are lined up to board the ferry than can fit on it. For this reason, the *Lady Alice* shares the route with another ferry, keeping a tight schedule between them: departing the west bank at Plaquemine on the hour and half hour and leaving the Sunshine landing on the quarter and three-quarter hour. It was a realistic timetable, since the river was not quite a mile wide between Plaquemine and Sunshine and a ferry crossing takes only six-and-a-half or seven minutes. It certainly offered more dependable service than in Mark Twain's day, when he observed that ferryboats "used to lose valuable trips because their passengers grew old and died, waiting."

Occasionally, ferries still get behind schedule. That's "because you have to worry about other vessels," Mike grumbled, reflecting the marine pecking order in which ferries lack priority. On our seventh crossing, I understood. We idled at the landing as he peered first through the windows and then at the radar screen. An upriver (northbound) tug and tow were steaming on, hugging the point near the far bank in order to avoid the worst of the current. "I'm going to leave early so I can beat him across," Mike said casually, noting that all cars wanting to cross were onboard. His description of "beating him across" made me a bit nervous, but Mike unfurled the radio cord and clicked on to broadcast. "Crossing over," he said emphatically, warning the tug captain that the *Lady Alice* would cross above—that is, upriver—from his vessel. It was a message that would carry to not only the tug captain but also any other boat within five miles. I heard the engines of the *Lady Alice* racing, powering up, and then we barreled out (as much as a ferry can) into the river. We arrived cleanly across the channel long before the tug had pulled abreast of the ferry landing. But Mike readily admitted that calculating when to cross before larger freighters and tankers required a different reckoning. Their deep drafts necessitate their staying in the deeper water of midchannel, a less predictable place.

The constant parade of boats was not Captain Mike's only challenge. He also must watch for large trees, loose buoys, and bulky trash, all of which ride downriver like rodeo stars on the current, whirling in eddies and creating potential hazards if they were to bash into the ferry. "We always try to go above boats, trees, and debris," Mike explained; it provides a more controlled crossing than a down-current run. Sometimes, if such a maneuver is needed, instead of steering the ferry in a straight diagonal from landing to landing, he directs the boat straight out and then turns—creating a right-angle ride instead of a path along the hypotenuse. Because of the current, however, he must always land the ferry facing upstream.

Throughout the morning, Captain Mike handled every landing in the same way: he moved the boat in sideways rather than nosing in, a technique called "walking the boat." It seemed to require a deft touch, working the sticks (what they call a ferry's steering mechanisms) to put the outside engine forward and the inside engine in reverse, a maneuver that must also consider the height of the river and the strength of the current. When the river is high and the current runs strong, "we let Mother Nature help," he smiled. "The current brings me in on the Plaquemine side [on the outside of a bend] . . . and if it's too fast I use the propellers. I consider both wind and current so I don't bump the dock too hard." And despite the morning's fierce winds and choppy river, he glided the boat into each landing so smoothly that it hummed to a stop with barely a tap. Only once did the wind or current get the better of him, requiring the *Lady Alice* to back into place. "This is called 'banking down,'" he offered, as if the miscalculation had been only to show me how to make the correction.

Captain Mike pointed out pre-set landing spots on each bank, which are calibrated to the height of the river. In all my rides, I'd never noticed them before. The loading apron must be moved along the bank with pulleys, adjusting to the bank and height of the river so that the boarding and debarking slopes are not too steep for automobiles. Sometimes, workers must shovel dirt under a landing to ensure that a pre-set landing is high enough.

Ferry schedules are tightly controlled, but a captain has the option of cancelling a run or more for cause—hazardous weather conditions such as fog or high wind, or mechanical problems. Some captains won't run in fog, Mike told me, although he usually would. But he is never rash, he is very careful, because he has a wife and four small children who wait for him in Plaquemine. And if a mechanical problem should arise, he always assumes he could find a substitute boat to make his run.

I rode back and forth all morning between the landings, but it was never boring; the views changed according to the light, and there was river traffic and activity on each bank. On more pleasant days, Mike told me, the banks bustle with fishermen and a few adventurers who putter in and out on the river in small boats. This day, because of the chill in the air and the brisk wind, people had stayed home, leaving the battures with only vegetation, the mechanical hardware of landings, and the flotsam that had washed ashore from upriver.

I will treasure my morning in Captain Mike's pilothouse. It is forever memorable and it will be even more so if the ferries are finally erased from the river. And I will probably always chuckle thinking about the ferryboat they called the *Lady Alice,* as a ferryboat that could just as easily have been named *Louisiana Floating Highway 75.*

❧ V ❧
Relicts of the "Peculiar Institution"

12

The Ironic History of Destrehan Plantation

The view from the second-floor gallery of Destrehan Plantation is lovely—a sweep of emerald lawn framed by leafy old live oaks and a backdrop of green levee that seems crowned with ruffled willows and blue sky. On the several occasions I've taken guests to see this oldest documented plantation home in the lower Mississippi River valley, I've asked the docent to linger here a bit.

I had enjoyed the view from this gracious porch several times before learning that in 1811, it had served as the venue for a tribunal of planters, including the eponymous Jean Noel Destrehan. They sat in judgment on the leaders of the just-quelled slave insurrection. As they overlooked a parterre garden of orange trees and herbs, the men solemnly directed that the captives be put to death and beheaded, and their heads be piked along the road. It was a procedure that modern legal scholars have suggested was anything but just.

The 1811 slave rebellion, now documented as the largest and bloodiest slave uprising in the history of the United States, took place on the east bank of the Mississippi River, along the so-called German Coast of the Territory of Orleans, now St. John the Baptist and St. Charles Parishes. Until recently, however, it was only a footnote to the better-known stories of Nat Turner's Virginia rebellion (1831) and John Brown's raid on Harper's Ferry, West Virginia (1859). Whispered tales from one generation to the next in the African American community and study by a few dedicated historians had kept the story alive. But it had generated little public awareness until the observance of the insurrection's bicentennial in 2011, when it came as a great surprise that such an event had happened in the neighborhood.

In 2005, Destrehan mounted a permanent exhibit to tell the story of the slave rebellion. It is a collection of colorful paintings and cut-out sculptures filled with energy and emotion, created by regional folk artist Lorraine Gendron. Viewed together as a narrative, they reflect the actions and consequences of the insurrection—harsh subject matter transformed into aesthetic pieces. To the exhibit, Destrehan has added a list of names of its slaves who participated in the revolt, detailing their place of birth, work on the plantation, and age. This roster effectively memorializes these individuals, who are otherwise lost to history.

When the Destrehan tour returns inside from the gallery, the docent pauses briefly at the door of a small office. It is cramped and furnished in a utilitarian manner, with period desks and chairs, an old wooden trunk, and a scattering of decorative pieces that convey a practical room of the mid-nineteenth century. The room lacks the same tastefulness that is apparent throughout the rest of the house. This room, says the docent, represents the short period of Destrehan's history when the plantation housed the Rost Home Colony, an agency of the Bureau of Refugees, Freedmen, and Abandoned Lands, better known as the Freedmen's Bureau. In 1865 and 1866, Destrehan was the venue where freed slaves came to participate in a benevolent program that assisted them in starting new lives.

I had taken the house tour several times before I was struck by the incongruity reflected by these two parts of Destrehan Plantation's history. In 1811, the plantation had been the site of severe and retaliatory treatment of slaves, in response to their futile attempt to win freedom. Merely two generations later, however, the same Destrehan was designated as a place of salvation and support for hundreds of emancipated slaves.

There was, of course, no linear connection between these two activities. Jean Noel Destrehan, one of the most prominent and powerful planters in the area, would have naturally been included in a high-profile event like the slave rebellion tribunal. And Destrehan Plantation's selection as headquarters for a home colony came only with the federal government's expropriation of Judge Pierre Adolph Rost's property, not because the judge had generously offered it.

Nevertheless, such a diametric reversal of purposes on the same plantation in such a short period of time seemed remarkable to me. And as I puzzled over the circumstance, I also wondered whether any of the newly freed residents who had come to the Rost Home Colony were descendants of the very slaves whose lives had been summarily terminated by the tribunal on the gallery.

I never found the answer to that question, but I saluted Destrehan for embracing both pieces of its history, irony and all.

The Louisiana slave rebellion was not a spontaneous expression of frustration and anger but as well-planned an undertaking as men and women living under the restrictions of slavery could manage. They had apparently been aware of the successful revolt in St. Domingue (now Haiti) in 1791, which had surely influenced their decision to organize for their own liberation. The River Road slaves held secret meetings, communicating among a string of plantations and with the maroons, runaway slaves living secretly—and freely—in small bands in nearby swamps and woods.

Leaders of the German Coast rebellion somehow knew that American forces based in New Orleans, the seat of the territorial government, were preoccupied with the Spanish in West Florida, making New Orleans more vulnerable to an attack. So the slave leaders devised a plan to capture the city by a two-pronged offensive: an army of slaves would march down the River Road gathering men and ammunition and then meet in New Orleans with a body of slaves who would have raided the arsenal there for weapons. Together, they would capture government offices and win their freedom.

Little is known about Charles, a mulatto recognized as the leader of the rebellion. He had been a driver (similar to an overseer) on the plantation of Manuel Andry, near what is now the town of LaPlace. On the evening of January 8, he led a small group of fellows to

Andry's home. The raid uncovered a disappointingly small cache of militia muskets, so they grabbed tools and implements such as cane knives, hoes, machetes, axes, and clubs. In the process, they wounded Andry and killed his son Gilbert.

This initial band of rebels set off through the cold and rainy night downriver along the River Road, joined by slaves from area plantations. As the group grew larger, they marched in formation, beating drums and waving battle flags under the rallying cry, "On to New Orleans!" The next afternoon, they halted at the plantation of Jacques Trepagnier (near present-day Norco), killed and cooked some of Trepagnier's poultry, and in misplaced exultation celebrated their march to freedom.

Meanwhile, terrified white planters in carriages and on horseback, some of them warned by their own slaves, had crowded the River Road, fleeing to New Orleans. The wounded Andry had escaped across the river, where he rallied a militia and sent word of the insurrection to territorial governor William C. C. Claiborne. The governor responded by ordering army troops from New Orleans and militia from Baton Rouge to move against the slaves, who, unaware of the forces mounting against them, continued their journey.

Rebels and troops encountered each other at Fortier Plantation but, as some later wrote, the attackers' metal weapons glinted in the moonlight as they took hiding places and the slaves fled into the woods, escaping back upriver. By daybreak, however, Andry arrived with the militia, and the well-armed contingent caught up with the poorly equipped slaves. The result, according to historian James H. Dormon, was "a mass execution, an open season on blacks in the vicinity."

By January 11, as Manuel Andry wrote Governor Claiborne, the insurrection had ended, its leaders killed or captured. Many of the slaves who had initially escaped were rounded up within the next several days; others fled into the swamps to join the maroons or secretly returned to their plantations.

Contemporary accounts of the rebellion estimated that between 150 and 500 slaves had participated in it, but no records exist to verify either number. And those figures did not include the slaves in

New Orleans. The River Road slaves had massed from twenty sugar plantations but ultimately traveled only twenty-five miles, having reached a place near the present location of the New Orleans airport. When the rebellion was thwarted, they were still a great distance from the seat of government in the Vieux Carré. As many as one hundred rebels were killed in the field; seventeen others were listed as missing or unaccounted for. The rebels had been severely outgunned and outmanned; as historian Robert Paquette has written, they "suffered such a quick and devastating defeat that their effort in retrospect might well look rather feeble."

A trial was held in New Orleans for some of the captured rebels, but the larger contingent was brought to Destrehan Plantation for trial. Judge Pierre St. Martin had invited Jean Noel Destrehan and four other planters to join him as a tribunal in proceedings that began on the afternoon of January 13. The hearing continued for two days, during which time thirty accused leaders were brought from a makeshift jail to face the jury. Many admitted their guilt. In fact, one slave told the panel that their purpose had been "*detruir le Blanc*" (to kill white people), which surely did nothing to soften the judges' hearts. However, recent historical research about the rebellion has concluded that the planters were more concerned with making the rebellion an example for other slaves than holding a session to mete out true justice.

The tribunal officially decreed that "the heads of the executed shall be cut off and placed atop a pole on the spot where all can see the punishment meted out for such crimes, also as a terrible example to all who would disturb the public tranquility in the future." They convicted twenty-one slaves, who were taken back to their respective plantations, shot, and beheaded. Two of Destrehan's slaves, the twins Gros and Petit Lindor, were executed on January 15 and their heads piked by the levee, perhaps just beyond the formal parterre garden of orange trees and herbs.

Casualties among planters and troops had numbered two: planters Gilbert Andry and Jean-Francois Trepagnier. No troops or militiamen were killed. In United States history, the 1811 slave rebellion was recognized as the first occasion when Federal troops were used in American territory to put down an insurrection. And in April 1811, the Louisiana Legislative Council passed an act providing compensation to planters for their lost property, specifically those slaves who had been killed or executed "on account of the late insurrection."

After the rebellion, Destrehan Plantation continued to flourish under Jean Noel's ownership. But with his death, the property became enmeshed in heirship complications; it was eventually purchased from one of Jean Noel's sons-in-law by another, Pierre Rost, a Frenchman, a lawyer and politician married to Louise Destrehan. Rost was responsible for having renovated the Creole mansion to classical revival elegance before he and his family moved their primary home to New Orleans, where he took a seat on the Louisiana Supreme Court. He continued to maintain Destrehan as a productive sugar plantation and summer home, but when the Civil War broke out, Rost's service to the Confederacy enabled him to accept a position as Confederate representative or ambassador to Spain. He and his family waited out the unpleasantness in Europe.

In 1862, the United States government seized properties of Confederate loyalists and those who refused to take an oath of allegiance to the Union. Rost's three properties—Destrehan, nearby Hermitage Plantation, and his home in New Orleans—were confiscated. The last was used as a school for black orphans, and Destrehan was placed under the Federal Bureau of Negro Labor, an agency that brought already-freed slaves to work the cane fields. The bureau suffered from gross mismanagement, however, and in May 1865, the newly formed Freedmen's Bureau took over the property.

Historian John Rodrigue has suggested that the Freedmen's Bureau was the first social welfare agency created by the American government, an exercise in idealism overseen by a military-style organization. In U.S. War Department Circular Order 29, Destrehan Plantation was converted to the Rost Home Colony, one of four such entities set up in Louisiana.

Home colonies were envisioned as self-supporting agricultural communities where "destitute refugees and freedmen" were given clothing, food, and supplies and trained and educated in matters financial, social, and political. The goal of the colony's program was to instill an understanding of the capitalist system and the values of competition in its residents.

Children under fourteen were required to attend school, but any able worker over fourteen years old was required to labor in various functions on the plantation, receiving pay or a share of the crops, which included sugarcane, cotton, corn, and sweet potatoes. Any profit left over from crop production in the extensive fields was used to help underwrite the expenses of the colony.

The Rost Home Colony would have been a bustling place. It had schools for its children and a resident doctor serving one of only three hospitals in the state that treated blacks. On the grounds was also a commissary, crop storage facilities, a cotton gin, a mill to process sugarcane into molasses, repair shops for equipment and tools, stores operated by the freedmen, and other necessities for running a small community.

The home colony's population peaked at approximately seven hundred men, women, and children, two hundred of whom had been slaves at Destrehan and another two hundred who had been at Rost's Hermitage Plantation. They occupied Destrehan's quarters cabins and more than two dozen newly built houses; some were assigned to live in Judge Rost's elegant mansion. Most of the home colony's residents were black, but a small percentage of them were impoverished white men, some married to black women. Some residents came only to receive medical care.

The Rost Home Colony was the only one of the four Louisiana home colonies that was successful, but it was terminated after less than two years. Judge Rost, returned home from Spain after the Civil War, had gained a pardon from a sympathetic President Andrew Johnson and filed an application to reclaim his properties. The application was granted. Rost reclaimed Hermitage Plantation and returned to live in his New Orleans home, but the Freedmen's Bureau negotiated an agreement to rent Destrehan for another year.

By late December 1866, however, the last residents of the home colony at Destrehan were transferred out, most to other Freedmen's

Bureau program sites; after another month, the home colony was officially closed, ending the brief period during which Destrehan Plantation had been dedicated to the betterment of freed slaves, compliments of the federal government. Pierre Rost never again lived at Destrehan, but he continued to operate the property as a sugar plantation with an overseer and freed laborers. In 1910, his descendants sold the plantation to an oil company, which in 1971 turned Destrehan over to the nonprofit River Road Historical Society, charged with preserving the house and interpreting its history.

The home colony program had ultimately proved much less successful than anticipated; the original concept had been for the emancipated slaves to apply for—and be granted—parcels of abandoned and confiscated lands. But most such properties, like those of Judge Rost, were returned to their original owners, so the freed slaves never achieved the status of independent entrepreneur.

Today, it is difficult to envision the Rost Home Colony at Destrehan because the grand mansion sits on a mere four acres, surrounded by burgeoning development. But I like to imagine it during that blink of history when these grounds buzzed with the activity of people whose lives seemed to hold promise for the first time.

Destrehan's staff does an excellent job conveying and interpreting the full history of this property, but I doubt they would agree that this history is ironic. They might rather conclude, with John Ruskin, that "there is no law of history any more than of a kaleidoscope," suggesting that I should not make a linear connection between the slave rebellion tribunal and the home colony in the context of Destrehan's history. They are, instead, random.

But as we know from Destrehan Plantation, sometimes the parts of a story can fit together in most unusual ways.

13

A Place with a Past Ever-Present

When I first visited Evergreen Plantation about fifteen years ago, it had only recently been opened to the public. Knowing that each River Road Plantation has a unique personality and an individual story to tell, I was curious to see what this one might offer. I couldn't tell much from the road; all I could see through its stately fence was a gracious white brick mansion with a curving staircase and a couple of white brick outbuildings set amid a sprawling green.

As I soon discovered, however, Evergreen is the only antebellum plantation in this area, and one of the few in the South, that survives essentially intact; its big house and a complement of dependencies, as such outbuildings are called in the lingo of plantation architecture, remain in place. Evergreen resembles those nineteenth-century paintings in which the artist portrayed a plantation as a small, almost self-sufficient village circumscribed by neat borders of sugarcane.

Here it was—in three dimensions.

So many antebellum properties along the River Road have been diminished over time, with buildings lost, moved, or destroyed. At Evergreen, however, little is missing: the old sugar mill was torn down in the 1920s and a post–Civil War Baptist church in the quarters was ruined during Hurricane Betsy in 1965. Otherwise, it is still much as it has been, including continuing to be a working sugar farm.

I followed a docent through the property, touring the big house that had begun life in the late eighteenth-century as a Creole farmhouse and that was updated to its classical revival appearance in 1832, following the architectural fashion of the time. I admired the contingent of surrounding buildings—pairs of garçonnieres and pigeonnairs, a kitchen, a milking barn, a carriage house, stables, the domestic slave house, a neoclassical privy, and I noted other structures, both older and newer, beyond the immediate orbit of the mansion.

But the most striking aspect of Evergreen's landscape was located some distance to the rear of the mansion complex. Down a long white shell drive lined with two-hundred-year-old moss-draped oaks is the elegantly somber layout of twenty-two nearly identical weathered cypress cabins. This is the Evergreen slave quarters, looking much as it would have when the last of them had been completed in the 1850s. Here, Evergreen's slave families and their free descendants lived until 1947.

I hadn't known that such a place still existed.

Slave cabins along the River Road are not unusual; I'd seen the small rustic buildings here and there, singly or in pairs, on the grounds of other plantations or relocated to a museum. But I'd never before seen a quarters whole and real. As I looked from the top of the cabin row down the shell road set beneath the sculptural oaks, it looked like a movie set. It is not. The Evergreen's quarters is authentic, confirmed by the only known historic map of the plantation, a rendering created by the Mississippi River Commission in 1876, which shows a configuration of Evergreen's buildings identical to what I saw, including the eleven slave cabins strung along each side of the road and encircled by identically placed fields of sugarcane.

That first visit had been in winter, when a leaden sky overhung the countryside and the palette of the landscape was muted. The weathered cabins, the color of dense smoke, crouched under gray tin roofs patinaed with rust and the muted greens of mosses. Even the short brick piers that supported each cabin seemed weathered to their own rusty color. The subdued colors, the elegant simplicity of the architecture, and the symmetry of the layout of the place made the quarters affecting, even a bit haunting, and I wandered slowly down the shell road beneath the oaks, surprised at its emotional power. But subsequent visits in more favorable weather have been equally affecting.

So I was not surprised to learn later from Jane Boddie, Evergreen's property manager, that my response was common. The intrinsic meaning of the quarters as a community of people, a village unto itself, often affects visitors—both black and white. No one, she told me, is able to avoid confronting the issue of slavery here, and some black visitors have even felt too uncomfortable to finish their tours. Conversely, some former residents have returned with their grandchildren, wanting to show them where they lived in the 1930s.

Slaves were critical to the life of this plantation, Jane Boddie told me, but the fact had been baldly conveyed by a document posted on the exterior of one of the cabins. This facsimile of the 1835 bankruptcy filing by owner Pierre Clidamant Becnel attests to the value of the slaves listed among his assets. They played key roles on the plantation: there was West, "an excellent blacksmith and engineer"; Joseph, a "Creole and cooper"; Gabriel, a "Creole and good carpenter and wheelwright"; Genevieve, a "Creole plantation cook"; and others who were master builders, blacksmiths, bricklayers, cabinetmakers, and field and domestic workers.

Pierre Becnel was a descendant of a German family who had arrived in what is now St. John the Baptist Parish in the eighteenth century and had consolidated tracts of smaller farms into a plantation. He had purchased Evergreen from his grandmother and had remodeled the old raised Creole cottage; at his bankruptcy, a cousin bought the property, and the extended Becnel family continued to live there. In 1893, Evergreen was sold to the Songys, another Creole family. They resided in the big house until 1930 after devastation from the 1927 flood and a destructive attack of mosaic disease to their sugarcane crop were compounded by the Great Depression. The bank foreclosed on the property and the Songys departed, leaving Evergreen empty and its buildings to face deterioration. Only the quarters cabins, though lacking running water and electricity, remained occupied by workers tending the fields.

Evergreen might have ultimately faced the fate of many other plantations—becoming derelict enough that demolition would follow—but for its good fortune in catching the eye of Louisiana oil heiress Mathilda Geddings Gray. She purchased the intact property in 1944 and began a thoughtful and extensive restoration of the buildings and grounds. Her vision has been continued and enhanced by her niece and successor.

When Mathilda Gray bought Evergreen, the twenty double cabins and two quadruple quarters cabins were still occupied by sugarcane workers. The structures, repaired and stabilized for more than a century and a half, now still retain much of their original construction—pegged beams, front facades of shiplap siding with traces of whitewash, doors that show the faded stain of the bright paints that once colored them, hearths and brick fireplaces on the shared wall that separated one family from another. But repairs had also been required; tin has replaced the original cypress shake roofs, and age-appropriate materials have been used to patch floorboards and walls, mantels, doors, and decorative transoms. When I peered into one of the tight twelve-by-twelve living spaces, I could not imagine the details of its residents' lives.

Because there is no written history by the slaves of what their lives were like, the management of Evergreen decided to investigate by sponsoring archeological digs in the quarters area. Clues emerged: ceramic shards and handmade nails were pulled from the layered dirt, as well as small toys, slate fragments from writing tablets, and buttons that might have been used for children's games or as voodoo totems. Behind the cabins were compressed areas revealing the sites of individual gardens and chicken coops.

These discoveries paralleled descriptions from other quarters along the river, described in memoirs of the era. Sir William Howard Russell, for example, visited the slave quarters at both Burnside and Oak Alley in 1863. At Burnside, he noted that "an avenue of trees runs down the centre of the negro street and behind each hut are rude poultry hutches which, with geese and turkeys and a few pigs [are a source of slave income]." He saw small patches of corn cultivated by the slaves that, with "five pounds of pork each week for each," supplied two of the staples in their diet. At Oak Alley he was led inside several cabins, where "the wardrobes . . . hang from nails or pegs driven into the wall. . . . Sometimes there is a table in addition to the plain wooden chairs, more or less dilapidated. . . . The ground 'round the huts was covered with litter and dust, heaps of old shoes, fragments of clothing and feathers amidst which pigs and poultry were recreating." Russell's host led him through the quarters, where, he wrote, they "broke in upon [the slaves'] family circle, felt their beds, and turned over their clothing." Russell felt like an intruder. "What right had I to do so?" he asked rhetorically in his account.

Eliza McHatton Ripley lived at Arlington, her family plantation, and wrote about the lives of their slaves. She noted their work as carpenters, coopers, masons, and sugar makers, and recorded that the quarters held a special infirmary for sick slaves and a day nursery for slave babies, who were tended by a grandmotherly slave. Slave families owned garden plots where they grew corn, cowpeas, and turnips, and their cabins were whitewashed inside and out each spring. Each living space included a fireplace equipped with a pot or skillet. The spiritual needs of Arlington's slaves were met by a moonlighting slave preacher who was the plantation's fulltime engineer.

At Evergreen, as elsewhere after the Civil War, freed slaves were offered the opportunity to remain in place; many stayed and continued to work. But they were paid for a time with script, exchangeable only at the Evergreen company store. Eventually, the occupants left for better opportunities; by 1947, the cabins were empty for the first time in more than a century.

Some say, however, that the spirits of these people still linger in Evergreen's quarters, and Joe McGill would agree. McGill visited Evergreen for the first time a couple of years ago, arriving not as a tourist like me but to spend the night. McGill, an African American who serves as a program officer at the National Trust for Historic Preservation, is the creator of the Slave Cabin Project, which he began in 2010, traveling about the South and obtaining permission to stay overnight in slave cabins. It was a way to honor the buildings' historic value and the contributions of the people who lived in them, but it is also effective in spotlighting the buildings, surviving in singles or pairs, and encouraging their owners to preserve them.

At Evergreen, McGill arrived too late to spur appreciation and preservation: to his delight "Evergreen has already done the right thing." So the night he spent there was in the company of twenty locals who had been invited to join him, to appreciate the singular experience of feeling the power of the quarters as the community it had been.

Joyce Jackson, an LSU professor of geography and anthropology, was among the guests who threw down their sleeping bags, yoga mats, and pillows on the creaky cabin floors to spend the night at Evergreen. Dr. Jackson, a clear-eyed scholar of African and African American culture, found the experience much more than a sleepover; it was, she remembered, amazingly spiritual. The evening began with group storytelling around a bonfire on the dark lawn in front of the big house and continued with a candlelit procession back to the quarters, where, in the flickering glow of torches, they remembered the ancestors—those at Evergreen and elsewhere. There was chanting, drumming, and the reading of slave stories, she told me, and some partook of an African ritual called libations, invoking memories by pouring liquids onto the ground while calling out names.

There were long pauses, Dr. Jackson said, and silences that evoked a deep solemnity. The night was slightly foggy and "you could see the high grass and trees behind the cabins." She looked at her surroundings and thought about the slaves of Evergreen, wondering if, on such a night a century and a half earlier, they would have been tempted to run off into the fog, seeking their freedom.

Through her daily responsibilities as property manager, Jane Boddie spends much of her time at Evergreen; but when she, too, joined McGill's event, she experienced the familiar place in a very different way. "I sat a little apart from the rest," she wrote in a testimonial for Joe McGill's blog about the Slave Cabin Project. "I wondered where I fit into all this. . . . I am white."

But she already knew the answer to her own musing. "If [these buildings] had all been destroyed, it would be hard to know where any of us fit, to remember who we are," she wrote. "We are a community of people. Past. Present. Future."

What Evergreen offers, as it guards its history and continues to preserve the intact plantation, is a clear and worthy link between them.

❧ VI ❧

Even the Products Have Stories

14

A Tale of Tobacco

And oh! Perique
Thy spicy essence speak;
In flowered roll enclose;
Thy incense fills
The aching soul instills
In gentle ease, repose.

—*New Orleans Times*, 1866

First, a disclaimer: I've never been a smoker and I believe implicitly in the Surgeon General's warnings about the unhealthy effects of tobacco and tobacco products. So it hurts me to confess that, despite this, I believe in perique tobacco. I love its rich and colorful tradition.

You are allowed to call me a hypocrite.

Perique has been grown and processed in St. James Parish for almost two hundred years and so comes with a legend and many traditions. Part of its legend holds that the crop will not grow anywhere else in the world but in the small alluvial triangle defined by a three-mile-wide base from Paulina to Belmont, tapering six miles north to the tiny, swamp-encircled community of Grand Point. The growing and processing of perique has been a tradition here for generations among a small number of families; the crop is still cultivated and cured much like it has always been.

The tobacco, too strong to smoke by itself but lauded for pipe blends, was a longtime international ambassador for Louisiana; aficionados swooned over the spicy sweetness it added to a pipe blend, calling it the "Champagne of tobaccos" after it won international competitions in 1875 at international expositions in Paris and Vienna.

Perique's story is colorful and long-lived. That its culture almost disappeared serves only to heighten my interest; I wonder why such an endemic product hasn't been more widely celebrated? There is no perique festival. Why aren't the economic development folks strewing around accolades extolling its global reputation?

Perique, the stuff of legend and tradition, probably deserves all that and more, but I still have qualms about extolling its virtues.

Legend has it that Acadian settler Pierre Chenet, nicknamed Perique, studied the ways that Louisiana's native Choctaws and Chickasaws cultivated and cured tobacco, then made small improvements to their techniques. By the 1820s, as the story goes, he had mastered the art sufficiently to found a small enterprise famously known as Tabac de Perique.

The Native Americans' secret was in their unique method of curing: they crammed tied bunches of dried tobacco leaves into a hollowed-out stump positioned near a well-selected tree and sealed the stump contents with a heavy cypress weight. They fitted a tall sapling into a low crotch of the tree branches and, using the sapling as a lever, applied pressure to the fitted top, then locked it in place. The pressure squeezed juice from the tobacco leaves, causing them to marinate and ferment in the stump. Several times during months of curing, the natives removed the leaves from the stump, aired them, and returned them under pressure. Chenet's enhancements included substituting wooden boxes for hollow logs and using a constructed frame instead of a sapling and notched tree. But the principles remained the same.

Historians who have investigated the perique story have suggested an alternate version, which muddies the legend slightly. When Christopher Columbus explored the New World, he discovered Taino natives on Hispaniola in the Caribbean smoking tobacco as a medicinal aid. Columbus carried the practice back to Europe, introducing tobacco to the Europeans in the late fifteenth century. It became very popular. When the colonial government encouraged their settlers in south Louisiana to start planting tobacco in the eighteenth century, those settlers might have cultivated the species now known as perique, brought in from the Caribbean. (Genetic analysis has revealed that perique is quite similar to some indigenous tobaccos in Dominica and Puerto Rico.) The Caribbean natives were also known to practice the process of fermentation under pressure. So the question arose: did colonial settlers actually bring the curing practices to Louisiana and share them with the natives?

Regardless of origin, however, cultivation of perique tobacco has been confined to this small area of St. James Parish and long ascribed to the singular properties of the soil. Minerals from a subterranean relic salt dome have leached into the surface soil, they say, creating a special environment for growing the tobacco. And it's true that when farmers tried growing perique elsewhere, including near other salt domes, they were never successful.

But, in truth, cultural influences rather than geography are more likely to have created the success of perique in this tiny corner of the world. Perique has always been a family business, and a family tradition, in which relatives and friends pitched in to help in the labor-intensive steps of sowing, harvesting, and processing the tobacco. Generations passed down their knowledge and trained their successors. Producing a fine perique, say the experts, is like trying to make the perfect gumbo—it's a hands-on art form.

The calendar for perique tobacco has not changed since Pierre Chenet adopted it from the Indians. Planting took place in late December or early January when seeds, so tiny that 100,000 are said to fit into a Cajun lady's sewing thimble, were mixed with wood ash and scattered in protected beds inside sheds or primitive greenhouses. Farmers nursed the seedlings until March or after the danger of frost had passed, covering them with palmetto leaves or grass to protect against nighttime chill, then baring them each morning to the sunlight. (Plastic sheeting eventually replaced palmetto leaves.) The best seedlings were transplanted by hand into prepared fields, which farmers tended with the usual apprehensions about threats to the crop—disease, insects, droughts, and deluges.

In early June, when the plants reached a certain size, family members marched through the fields to pinch off the suckers—top growths—to encourage larger, fuller leaves at the bottom of the stalk. Harvest came during the sweaty months of June and July, when farmers hacked the base of each stalk by hand with a machete or a cane knife and left the plants overnight to wilt on the rows. The following morning, they gathered the plants and took them to the barn, where each stalk was individually pierced with a nail and hung over wires to dry, a process called airing. After two weeks, the stiff forest-green leaves had become limp brown foliage, ready for processing.

The dried tobacco leaves were then moistened and heaped before women and children, who undertook the time-consuming ritual of stripping the unusable stems away from the leaves, then tying the leaves into bundles called carottes, which were jammed into containers. Originally these were Chenet-type curing boxes, but they were replaced in the 1920s by oak barrels, comparable to whiskey barrels. The sealed containers were put under pressure, at first with levered saplings until the introduction of ballast stones piled onto the container lids in the mid-nineteenth century. (Louisiana has no natural rocks; these stones arrived in the bellies of ships, having been placed there to keep them stable in open water, but they were not required for traveling on the Mississippi River.) In the 1920s, ballast gave way to screwjacks, a more efficient, mechanical way to apply pressure. But regardless of the equipment, at several intervals during the year of curing, the tobacco was pulled from its containers, laid on boards to air, then returned to containers to continue fermenting. One visitor in 1892 arrived at a tobacco shed while the perique was airing and described it as "rope-twisted and looking like a section of weather-beaten Atlantic cable."

In early fall, containers of tobacco were hauled to a dealer, who cured it further—measured in months or years, depending on the desired strength, and then sold it, often blended with selected Kentucky tobaccos. Although New Orleans dealer S. Hernsheim Brothers

& Company first dominated the perique market, within a short time three St. James Parish merchants began to compete. Christophe Roussel, Louis Aristee Poche, and J. F. Guglielmo became prominent perique dealers—financing farmers, buying their tobacco and further processing it, then negotiating its sale. They fiercely contended among themselves, were proprietary about their farmers, and equally secretive about their customers.

Guglielmo's and Roussel's companies were based in Paulina; Poche's company was headquartered in Convent. Each received orders for perique with postmarks from across the United States and around the world: New York, Chicago, Boston, San Francisco, England, Switzerland, Sweden, Germany, and beyond. L. A. Poche's 1937 company letterhead listed his offices in New Orleans and Convent and detailed the scope of his business: "High grade Louisiana 100% Perique. Exporter. Large storage facilities for those who wish to buy in advance to protect against crop failure."

At its peak in the 1950s, a mere 1,100 acres of perique were planted among the 25,000 acres of St. James Parish sugarcane. But the tobacco was sought after by "the lowly and the great," bragged an article in a 1945 *St. Jamesian* magazine, mentioning that "just a few weeks ago, the Louisiana Perique Tobacco Company at Lutcher made a gift of the tobacco to [Josef Stalin] the Soviet commander, some in cut form and some in carrottes." Perique was interesting enough to a national audience in 1955 for the venerable *Saturday Evening Post* to print an extensive article about the tobacco and its culture. Approximately one hundred farmers grew the crop at that time.

But perique's bright future soon began to dim. By the late 1960s, the number of farmers planting tobacco had diminished to twenty-five; in 1979, only 150 acres were planted in perique. In the 1980s, the industry had weakened so dramatically that Roussell and Guglielmo shuttered their businesses, leaving Poche as the last perique dealer in the world.

What caused the demise of perique tobacco? The decline of pipe smoking was one of the reasons given, but it was more likely the effect of other influences. High taxes on tobacco couldn't have helped, but the labor-intensive nature of perique farming and processing was the most likely cause. By the 1960s, the younger generation of St. James families much preferred working in local chemical plants instead of farming tobacco, choosing to raise soybeans and sugarcane if they farmed. By the 1990s, only one full-time perique famer remained in St. James Parish; others who continued to plant the tobacco did so avocationally, loyal to the tradition.

It seemed as if Pierre Chenet's enterprise was on the verge of extinction.

And then, quite suddenly, perique's future began to brighten, thanks to a couple of unlikely white knights who arrived from out of state. The first, a southwest specialty tobacco company, had learned of perique when the last full-time farmer, desperate to save his business, mailed samples of his product to an array of potential buyers. The company recognized the potential of adding the spicy tobacco to its cigarettes and in 2000 contracted with the elderly farmer and his family for their crop. Since then, more farmers have been enticed to grow perique for the cigarette maker.

In 2005, a self-assured tobacco man from North Carolina arrived in St. James Parish. Mark Ryan wore coke-bottle glasses, pinched an ever-present cigar between his lips, and had no idea who Pierre Chenet was or that perique was a venerable tradition. He did, however, own a tobacco company and had a good nose for the business, buying the L. A. Poche Perique Tobacco Company and inheriting Poche's longtime manager, Curtis Hymel. With Hymel's help, Ryan set about to resurrect the dying business.

Mark Ryan operated from a base of optimism and vision, since his new acquisition included inadequate processor buildings and presses and no stock of fermented tobacco ready to sell. After he began to stabilize the business, he then courted heresy by introducing a bundle of newfangled farming and processing techniques to the perique triangle for the few farmers still planting acreage. These were best practices, already established in other tobacco-growing areas, but new to perique farmers who had had been out of touch with the industry for over thirty years. Ryan said he wanted to put them back in the game.

He refurbished Poche's barns, which dated from 1933 and 1973, and added a new 20,000-square-foot building equipped with receiving bays, refrigerated storage, and a large bright air-conditioned space for stripping and bundling the tobacco in comfort. He planned to operate his facility nine months of the year, not just in season. And in 2009, in the greatest break with local tradition, Ryan offered to buy the dried tobacco directly from the farmers. This would save them the time and effort required in the arduous steps of hand-stripping the leaves and fermenting. (Leaves do not have to be stripped from stems if used in cigarettes.) His offer wasn't entirely a goodwill gesture, Ryan confessed; a new federal law required that a tobacco processor must have a license, so any farmer with a barn, barrels, and no permit would have been deemed illegal.

As he began to attract farmers back to growing perique, Ryan introduced a number of progressive techniques: pH testing in the fields, for example, to minimize the use of fertilizer and cut costs; new irrigation techniques; sending perique seeds to be coated in order to produce uniform seedlings that farmers could use in new hydroponic planting processes in new greenhouses, producing a larger crop of transplantable seedlings. He also arranged to sell some of his tobacco to the specialty cigarette manufacturer, which increased the market for his growers. Despite the customary belief that perique had never been used in cigarettes, it was whispered to have been the secret ingredient that gave New Orleans–branded Picayune cigarettes their legendary kick when they were enjoyed by adventurous smokers from the late 1890s until the 1960s.

Mark Ryan was also a showman with numerous contacts in the industry; he attended pipe shows and tobacco conventions, talked up his new product, and interested industry magazines in his story. Suddenly, after fifty years, media began paying attention to perique tobacco again. Just six years after this second newcomer arrived, people in St. James Parish began to notice that their traditional crop was coming back. Planted acreage for perique had quadrupled; even a few members of the disaffected younger generation had decided to give perique farming a try. And, with good-humored heresy, Ryan contracted a farmer to plant perique in Vacherie, on the west bank of the

Mississippi River, beyond the traditional magic triangle. The river had wandered all over the place, Ryan told me, and geologists believe that it split the formation called the Vacherie Salt Dome. So why wouldn't the land on the west bank be just as good for perique farming; he decided to give it a try.

In short, Ryan's practices were unorthodox, and very liberating.

Grant Martin is the third generation of perique farmers selling to L.A. Poche, which puts him in Mark Ryan's stable of farmers. Martin has farmed perique part-time in the family's Grand Point fields, just because he'd promised his father he'd keep it going. His full-time job is in local banking. His brother Gene, his partner in perique, works in the petrochemical industry.

I met Grant Martin as he rolled on a large John Deere tractor through twenty acres of broad, leathery, deep green leaves. His crop of 50,000 plants had firm stalks about three feet tall that he sprays for worms; if the weather is just right, he told me, he can also use the tractor and sprayer to kill suckers. This would be a great boon to Martin and his six field workers, who would otherwise have to do it the traditional way—by hand. Under the Ryan regime, the Martins have put more acres into perique cultivation than they have had for a very long time. And Grant Martin isn't sorry that after cutting and drying his tobacco, he can haul the crop to Poche, get paid, and know that his family is free from the laborious steps required in stripping and curing the perique.

The L. A. Poche Tobacco Company is a small unpretentious complex separated from the River Road by a dirt parking area. The barn smelled sweet and earthy, probably little different than its smell fifty years ago. Rows of oak barrels, striped with abstract black lines from decades of dense black tobacco juice, were arranged along a platform. Atop each barrel was a stalwart metal screwjack that required two muscular men, straining, to pull its lever and ratchet up pressure on the tobacco fermenting within the barrel. Some of the oak barrels wore white cloth caps, like the calico tied onto the lid of jelly jars at a county fair. They indicate that the tobacco in those barrels is ready for sale, manager Curtis Hymel told me.

The sound of a loud metallic clank rang out as a worker removed the jack from a barrel; he reached in to lift two hefty black weights from the contents, then pulled strands of fermenting perique from the barrel. It was dense, limp, and black as he laid it, like oil-coated seaweed, to air on a long wide board. After a few more such airings, the 500-pound contents of the barrel will be ready to sell.

In Ryan's new industrial building at the rear of the complex, loud music blared as teams of men and women processed heaps of tobacco. Some of the women straddled chairs in front of bales of chocolate-brown tobacco the size of doghouses, pulling out stalks and tying them into bouquets that were carried to a dedicated corner and washed. Then they are returned for hand-stripping and packing into the oak barrels. In North Carolina, Ryan told me, large tobacco processors use expensive steaming machines to dampen and strip the tobacco, but that state-of-the-art processing may never come to St. James Parish. "This is a very expensive crop," said the Poche Company's new owner. "It may be the most valuable crop per acre that's grown." Then Mark Ryan shrugged and smiled around his cigar. "I am the now the biggest private business in the parish," he said. "I saved perique."

Purists have objected to the many changes that have encroached on the St. James Parish perique traditions. This new business is quite different from what Pierre Chenet began, or even how it was practiced in the 1960s. I won't argue with the purists; they're correct. But I also believe that the introduction of modern techniques and equipment may have saved this segment of local culture that had been threatened with becoming nothing but a museum exhibit.

Now, St. James perique—the product—will remain part of the River Road, at least for the foreseeable future. I'm still sorry it's a tobacco, of course, but it's our tobacco and I'm glad our tradition lives on.

15

Anatomy of a Company Town

Through the years, I'd peered through the fences encircling Colonial Sugars in Gramercy with a growing curiosity. I wondered why this plant didn't resemble other manufacturing complexes along the River Road. Of course, it had the traditional industrial geometry of pipes and steel, but within its defining fences were also a block of comfortable old frame houses shaded by giant sycamores, the shell of a brick church, and an open grassy space that might once have been a park. It seemed rather unusual for an industrial site and, as I eventually learned, it was.

Colonial Sugars is the surviving landscape of a company town that not only retains its original setting but also has its central factory still in operation, surrounded by a representative sampling of its original, and now historic, buildings. In the late nineteenth and early twentieth centuries, company towns were common developments, enabling manufacturing facilities in rural areas like St. James Parish to ensure they had a dependable workforce. They provided not only employment and housing but also, depending on management's disposition, an array of amenities. Colonial Sugars was not unusual. Other River Road company towns included Cinclare in West Baton Rouge Parish and Godchaux in Reserve, both sugar processors; Garyville, Lutcher, and White Castle, all established by lumber companies. Today, however, Colonial Sugars is unique along the River Road and is also the only sugar company town that still exists in the United States.

Because of this, in 1995 the complex was entered on the National Register of Historic Places. This certification acknowledged that despite numerous changes to the property wrought over the century by hurricanes, building relocations and renovations, enough remained to evoke the historic flavor and spirit of place of the Colonial Sugars company town. My view through the fence had been of a place even more unusual than I'd imagined—a place I wanted to understand. And that, I decided, should entail a visit inside, as well as finding former residents to tap for their memories.

The former proved more difficult than I expected. I knew Colonial Sugars is never open to the public and my several attempts to cajole my way past its guarded gate had been notably unsuccessful. So I set about calling a roster of company administrators to request a tour, as a way to appreciate their historic property. No one was sympathetic, until after a frustrating sequence of negative responses, I happened finally on a sympathetic ear with the authority to grant me entry, for the sake of history. Yes, I could come see what remained of the company town on the property now officially known as the Louisiana Sugar Refining LLC (LSR).

That was how, on a hot summer morning, I found myself standing outside the Colonial Sugars visitor center awaiting my guide and inhaling the unfamiliar pulsing atmosphere of a large industrial complex. I watched as a phalanx of golf carts whipped past along North Fifth Avenue, ferrying people in navy blue company shirts to and from unmatched buildings, weaving bravely through a parade of slowly rolling eighteen-wheelers. At the end of the block, I noted a stalled hopper car protruding into the road; trucks, golf carts, and bicycles veered around it. Later, I learned it was the last of a string of railroad cars parked beneath a loader.

The air was permeated with a distinctive odor—thick, pungent, and unfamiliar, and unseen machinery growled, providing a loud white noise broken by the occasional shriek of a whistle slicing through the baritone hum. Overhead, billows of white steam shot in rhythmic bursts from tall thin stacks near another double stack that towered above the complex and bore iconic symbols: a blue Colonial Sugars logo; above that, a red and blue X imprinted "Dixie Crystals" in white; and the whole capped by a white oval sunburst proclaiming "Made in Louisiana."

I was mesmerized by the dynamism of the place when Mandy, a young woman wearing a blue company shirt and a big smile, puttered up in a golf cart. She had local roots, I learned later, and an appreciation for Colonial Sugars' history and had been sent to show me around. But her cheery greeting came with an effusive apology: she would not be able to include the refinery building on our tour. I hid my very real disappointment, having been fascinated by processing tours since a third-grade field trip to the Godchaux Refinery. But I smiled and nodded, grateful enough to be on the other side of Colonial Sugars' fence.

In 1895, Faubourg Lapin (Rabbit Town) was a community of one hundred residents who claimed a wheelless boxcar as a train station and had to travel five miles upriver to the nearest church. But a group of New York investors in the Yazoo and Mississippi Valley Railroad decided they needed something to fill up their empty north-bound boxcars, so they founded the Gramercy Sugar Company, renaming Rabbit Town after their home neighborhood, Gramercy Park in Manhattan. The new plant began to attract workers from the immediate area and beyond, tripling the local population.

Their venture began as a mill that crushed and ground sugarcane but its owners soon added a refinery and began buying up surrounding plantation properties. By 1904, their investment had become a splendid model of vertical integration—6,400 acres of fields, on which they raised sugarcane that they then both milled and refined into the familiar granulated product we spoon into coffee. The mill closed in 1914, but the refinery has continued to operate ever since, through numerous changes in company names and managements and the requisite additions of updated machinery.

The most recent change occurred in 2010 when the complex became LSR, owned through a joint venture between two giant out-of-state corporations—Imperial Sugar and Cargill—and the Louisiana

Sugar Growers and Refiners Association. This offered the latter group, a consortium of eight hundred cane farmers and eight existing sugar mills, a piece of the refining endgame for the first time in the two-hundred-year history of the Louisiana sugar industry. The new management also replaced the century-old refining building with a new refinery, a sleek metallic box that crouches on the vintage landscape like a modernist sculpture and houses state-of-the-art equipment for the complicated multistep refining process.

In its heyday, Colonial Sugars was considered a large and extended family, where, a local newspaper observed, the average employee worked for over twenty years, several generations in a family often worked there together or successively, and 90 percent of employees lived in company housing. But Colonial's management provided much more than housing. Then, no fence encircled the town where company-sponsored schools—segregated by race—educated children to the seventh grade; a company-run general store offered shopping on credit; and company recreational facilities included a movie theatre, a swimming pool, a park, a baseball park, and a nine-hole golf course. Residents could attend the Catholic church located on the grounds, buy stamps at the company post office, and have everyday medical problems tended by a company doctor. Residents' lives revolved around loud whistle blasts like the one I'd heard while waiting for Mandy, blaring three times daily to signal shift changes and anytime, day or night, to alert the community to an accident, a fire, or some other emergency. It was the kind of place where an employee on a bicycle rounded up and delivered lunch boxes from individual homes to workers on their midday break.

Colonial Sugars supplied and purified its own running water (brought in from the river), generated its own steam and electricity, and maintained a set of shops to fix whatever broke. It owned and operated a telephone system and furnished a sewerage system for the complex before most other local communities had anything comparable.

The company town structure endured into the 1960s, ending when it no longer needed to endure the headaches of administering a community as well as running a sophisticated manufacturing facility. Some have suggested it ended because of a dramatic strike that altered the relationship between the management and labor; others offered that federal desegregation laws had altered the social landscape. But at least part of the impetus for abandoning the company town structure was simply that area population had grown significantly and there was ample workforce for the plant.

Mandy aimed the golf cart down North Fifth Avenue toward several of the most historic industrial buildings. She pointed out the landmark nine-story red brick char house that has loomed over the property since 1902, in which twenty-foot-high cisterns once filtered the brown color from liquefied sugar. The classically handsome, utilitarian lines of the building are visible from a distance, but only up close could I see that its façade was pocked with squinting windows of broken glass. It is no longer in use, Mandy acknowledged, and was so well built that even after a serious fire in 1969, only its wood floors and supports were damaged. It remains structurally sound and, I hoped, eligible for a creative new use.

Facing North Fifth Avenue in the shadow of the char house is the property's most famous building, the neoclassical brick and concrete boiler house, which has a front façade decorated with a tiny wrought-iron balcony with imposing letters engraved across its architrave: COLONIAL.SUGARS.COMPANY. The boiler house, built in 1929, had been designed by McKim, Mead, and White and is only one of two buildings in the state by one of the most elite New York–based architectural firms of its day. No one seems to know why these prominent architects had come to design a building for a sugar plant in rural Louisiana. Perhaps one of the New York investors had known them, or perhaps it was because both Charles McKim and Stanford White had once worked with Henry Hobson Richardson, another nationally acclaimed New York architect who had grown up in St. James Parish just across the Mississippi. Whatever the reason, the boiler house has brought Colonial Sugars positive attention in historic architectural circles for decades.

Just across the narrow main street from the boiler, Mandy pointed out a small gray stucco building with a neoclassical portico and a span of multipaned windows. It looked like a poorly planned bungalow but is actually the power house, originally constructed in 1909 to produce steam power for the plant's operation and still in use today.

Our golf cart whipped between two behemoth eighteen-wheelers and behind the hopper cars, across railroad tracks that have bisected Colonial Sugars property since its founding. According to Merrill Gerstner, one of the former residents of the company town, those tracks played a major role in everyone's daily life. People planned when they could travel unimpeded from one end of the complex to the other according to the schedule of the trains. His sister Gretchen Bankston remembered hobos occasionally emerging from the freight cars and wandering the streets of the town, seeking work or food before going on their way.

Beyond the railroad tracks, several cozy-looking cottages remain. They are painted cream with moss-green trim and have small front porches, the only survivors of a large residential area of almost seventy cottages built between 1910 and 1917 along South Fifth Street as well as along Fourth, Third, and Second Streets and Central Avenue. Robert Montelius remembered the area as New Town, where the blocks were divided between workers' and supervisors' homes. After the company town disbanded, residents bought and moved their cottages, which left a broad swath of open land on which the monumental new refinery building ultimately arose.

Lorraine Oubre was born in 1927 in one of the cottages. She remembered that they had been available in two models. Her family's home was L-shaped with three bedrooms, one bath, a screened back porch with a washing machine, and a small back yard. Her house was located just two lots away from the company school for white children, the first public school in Gramercy, where children of company executives and laborers and even townies from off-property attended. The school was, she recalled, a comfortable frame building raised high on brick pillars so that on rainy days, the broad paved area under the building became a fine dry playground.

Colonial Sugars' black workers lived north of the plant across Main Street in a separate residential neighborhood with its own company school. The company-built cottages looked very much like those of the white workers, Lorraine Oubre remembered. Today, neither school building nor any of the black workers' cottages survive in place.

Tree-shaded Park Avenue, also known as Executive Row, was distinct from New Town. Colonial Sugars' executives and their families lived in the comfortable old frame houses I'd seen through the fence. At one time, the long block held an unbroken line of residences, a duplex with guest apartments, and a boarding house. Now grassy lots separate the remaining buildings, creating a gap-toothed welcome around Blue House, the most historic of the old homes.

Blue House (now painted white) continues as the nickname for the old President's House. It is a gracious-looking Eastlake-style house built in 1910 with a broad front gallery leading into a surprisingly compact and practical interior. The house has undergone many refurbishments through the years, Mandy told me. Today, it is the official venue for entertaining LSR guests and for holding official company meetings, but I still thought I could sense the presence of its most colorful resident, George P. Meade.

Meade was president of Colonial Sugars from 1923 to 1956; he was also coauthor of the definitive *Cane Sugar Handbook* and internationally recognized in the sugar industry. One of his hobbies was collecting reptiles, which he kept in a 1,500-square-foot enclosure in the back yard. His menagerie included nonpoisonous snakes, turtles, and an alligator named Smokey, all of which stayed behind when Meade retired and moved to the Pontchartrain Hotel in New Orleans. The pets were adopted by Merrill Gerstner and Gretchen Bankston, children of Meade's successor, George Gerstner. They also inherited visits from directors of prestigious American zoos, such as those in San Diego and St. Louis, who had come at Meade's invitation to use Colonial Sugars as a base for their specimen collecting visits. A surprised Merrill Gerstner was invited to tag along on their outings to the nearby swamps and remembered them fondly.

Executive Row was reserved for the company's top administrators, although, confessed Lorraine Oubre, her family lived there too, right on the corner of Park Avenue and South Fifth Street. Her father worked in the lab; he was not an executive. But President Meade had somehow gotten to know him and liked him, and when he learned that the family of two parents and thirteen children was crowded into one of the workers' cottages, he had them relocated them to more spacious quarters.

Company workers arrived at the homes on Executive Row to do yard work, tend the large gardens, change light bulbs, and take care of house repairs. Local farmers pulled their trucks up to the back doors of Park Avenue homes to offer the lady of the house seasonal vegetables, and on Fridays local fishermen and seafood vendors came to hawk their freshest catches for Catholic families observing a meatless day.

At the far end of Park Avenue, beyond the executive houses, stood the company store. The large frame building had a broad front porch that opened into an expansive room with aisles of stacked shelves, a creaky wood floor, and a post office tucked into a rear corner. The store offered dry goods and a limited selection of groceries, but at the end of each month, the children of Colonial Sugars came to claim a lagniappe gift from the store clerk after their previous purchases had been deducted from their fathers' paychecks. The store closed in 1948, a victim of competition from retailers beyond the company, but the Gramercy post office and a local credit union continued to use the space until the building was razed in 1981. Today, it is a graveled lot with LSR offices in gray trailers.

Across Park Avenue from the company store was the company clubhouse, also a raised frame building painted a memorable burgundy color. Its wide front porch led to a large windowed room that overlooked shady green Gramercy Park. The ladies of Colonial Sugars considered the clubhouse an ideal venue for their meetings and social gatherings such as the bridal shower of Lorraine Oubre's sister.

At that time, the park was planted with shade trees, palms, and flowering shrubs, and along the length of its back border was an immaculately trimmed hedge to separate the park from the railroad tracks. The park belonged to the community—it was the place where children ran and played, families strolled, and the company held its annual May Day festival. This was a much-anticipated event when school children danced their practiced steps around a maypole, bands played lively tunes, and everyone clamored to go home with a cake from the extensive bake sale.

In the far corner of Gramercy Park was the church, the distinctive shell I'd seen through the fence. The building had been constructed in 1910 as the meeting hall for a chapter of Woodmen of the World, but its tall red brick walls and expansive windows made it easily transformed into a Catholic church after the Woodmen moved elsewhere. The archdiocese had requested that Colonial sell or, better yet, donate the building to them; when Colonial Sugars countered with only a lease offer, negotiations collapsed into a standoff until 1920, when the Sacred Heart of Jesus Mission Chapel opened in the stately hall. It offered Mass every morning before the six o'clock shift and barred children from its second floor, where the men gathered to play pool. In 1955, when a large new Catholic church was built in the town proper of Gramercy, the chapel was deconsecrated and used as a community center, then as a warehouse. Now its tall windows are boarded, its belfry cropped, and its future uncertain.

At the opposite end of the park was the company town's Olympic-size swimming pool, which was for many years the only such facility between New Orleans and Baton Rouge. The Colonial Sugars' competitive swim team was one of the most popular activities for children of all ages, and team members trained long hours in order to hold their own against big-city swimmers from City Park and Audubon Park in New Orleans. According to a *Times-Picayune* story in 1925, Colonial Sugars hosted one such meet where "the local boys showed good spirit and gameness against the New Orleans stars in spite of the evident superiority of the visitors." President Meade, who was a great booster of the swim team, graciously overlooked his team's loss and invited all the competitors for dinner. Five years later, the *Picayune* reported that Meade was elated when Colonial Sugars was chosen to host an international swimming competition.

When the pool was filled in during the early 1970s, the once-gracious park lost its last distinguishing feature. By that time, its plantings had been removed, leaving a bare and open greensward.

Mandy's tour of the historic district did not include a spin across

River Road to see the landing where sugar has been offloaded from ships since the early twentieth century. Nor did we penetrate the warren of buildings in the old industrial core, although I knew from having read Colonial Sugars' application to the National Trust that the complex harbored significant early industrial structures that delighted preservation historians. These included steel filter tanks dating from 1908, a heavy-timbered storeroom built in 1905, a fire pumper house from 1900 and the so-called U and Y processing buildings, standing since 1895.

Instead, our golf cart breezed past a cluster of huge squatty tanks that Mandy identified as storing cane juice or second-grade molasses and pulled to a stop before the broad open doorway of a hulking, pyramid-shaped corrugated metal warehouse. I peered into its dimly lit cavern that seemed as long as a football field and spotted a dwarf front loader poking at the flank of a buff-colored hill at the far end. This was a mountain of raw sugar, but the scale of both the building and the mass of sugar was so monumental that I had mistaken the full-size machine for a toy. And this was just one of several warehouses that had been in use at Colonial Sugars since before 1920.

Warehouses had been off-limits to company town children except for Christmas Eve. Then, the company transformed one of them into the site of an annual children's Christmas party. Prior to the occasion, every employee had obtained a ticket for each of his children; at the party, every child was called up to a large stage by age group where an enthroned Santa Claus greeted them and bestowed presents. For one magical evening, a cavernous sugar warehouse echoed with the voices of hundreds of delighted children in party clothes.

The warehouse marked the official end of Mandy's tour, and she spun the golf cart around, retracing our path toward the visitor center. As we crossed the complex, I could almost imagine what the Colonial Sugars Historic District must have looked like when it was not yet part of history but the home of busy people in a bustling company town. And I had to acknowledge enormous respect for the extensive organization that must have been required to plan, build, and maintain a community while simultaneously operating a sophisticated industrial complex.

Before I departed through the guarded gate, I glanced up once more at the iconic double stack soaring above the rooftops and realized that its lettering, though still legible, was extremely faded: *Colonial Sugars* and *Dixie Crystals* and *Made in Louisiana,* almost a shorthand history of the place, could barely be read. It was a visual image that I hoped was not symbolic—that the long and colorful story of Colonial Sugars would not fade away too. It easily could, of course, because inclusion in the National Register, though important, holds no guarantee for protection of the designated buildings. Owners of such properties may generally do what they wish, and Mandy had casually mentioned that many of the old buildings could eventually be demolished.

After my visit to the Colonial Sugars Historic District, I knew that it would never rival Colonial Williamsburg, the famous living history village in Virginia. But the sugar complex, unique along the River Road as well as within the United States, deserves appreciation. As I drove away, I silently offered good wishes to LSR for a long and successful future in the business of refining sugar, even as I also fervently hoped that the remnants of its company town would always continue to be part of it.

ACKNOWLEDGMENTS

When I approached LSU Press with the idea of writing a collection of essays about the River Road featuring places and aspects that I deemed unique or underappreciated, MaryKatherine Callaway, the director of the Press, enthusiastically encouraged me. I should thank her for committing me to the most challenging project I've ever undertaken. It was premised on personal experience, but I determined it would be more interesting with the addition of archival research and interviewing people whose first-hand information and background was more complete than my own, whose insights would enrich the stories.

Tracking down the right people was sometimes difficult and I was forced to abandon two subjects when I couldn't get the responses I needed or inveigle individuals into allowing me to use their information.

Nevertheless, I am eternally grateful to the following people who did share what they knew about their subjects. In a very real sense, they get credit as my ghostwriters:

Mandy Capella, Red Guerts, Gretchen Bankston, Lorraine Oubre, Merrill Gerstner, Robert Montelius; Grant Martin, Mark Ryan, Curtis Hymel, Ken Guidry, Donal F. Day; Delos Turner; Peter Patout, Susan Turner, Scott Purdin, Kevin Risk; Hazel Taylor, John Rodrigue, Michael Knight; Bill Stegelmeyer, Mark Gautreau, Jay Lemann, Stuart Rockoff; Andrew Capone; Glenn Falgoust; Sam Bacot; Clifford Normand, Gene LeBlanc, David Broussard; Simeon Peterson, Elizabeth Schexnyder, Jim Krahenbuhl, Andi Bahlinger, Diane Follmer; Sidney Marchand, Jay Lemann; Virginia Noland, Claude Reynaud; Father Frank Uter, Father Vincent J. Dufresne; Charlie Duhe, Joe Samrow; Kathe Hambrick-Jackson; Andrew; Jane Boddie, Joseph McGill, Joyce Jackson.

I am indebted, as always, to the professional and efficient

librarians who saved me inordinate amounts of time by helping find relevant material much more quickly than I could have done so independently. Among the best were Marc Wellman, Louisiana State Library, and Tara Laver and Judy Bolton, Hill Memorial Library at LSU.

And I continue to be grateful to my family for asking how I was doing and cheering me on when I seemed to be slogging through instead of skating along. For inspiration and constant support—thank you all!